Martin Luther King

# I have a dream

## words to change the world

- MOTIVATE your pupils to write and appreciate poetry.
- INSPIRE them to share their hopes and dreams for the future.
- BOOST awareness of your school's creative ability.
- WORK alongside the National Curriculum or the high level National Qualification Skills.
- Supports the *Every Child Matters - Make a Positive Contribution* outcome.
- Over £7,000 of great prizes for schools and pupils.

"When I was out there I was never ever alone, there was always a team of people behind me, in mind if not in body."
Ellen MacArthur

# West Yorkshire
## Edited by Mark Richardson

 Young**Writers**

First published in Great Britain in 2006 by:
Young Writers
Remus House
Coltsfoot Drive
Peterborough
PE2 9JX
Telephone: 01733 890066
Website: www.youngwriters.co.uk

All Rights Reserved

© Copyright Contributors 2006

SB ISBN 1 84602 511 7

# Foreword

Imagine a teenager's brain; a fertile yet fragile expanse teeming with ideas, aspirations, questions and emotions. Imagine a classroom full of racing minds, scratching pens writing an endless stream of ideas and thoughts . . .

. . . Imagine your words in print reaching a wider audience. Imagine that maybe, just maybe, your words can make a difference. Strike a chord. Touch a life. Change the world. Imagine no more . . .

'I Have a Dream' is a series of poetry collections written by 11 to 18-year-olds from schools and colleges across the UK and overseas. Pupils were invited to send us their poems using the theme 'I Have a Dream'. Selected entries range from dreams they've experienced to childhood fantasies of stardom and wealth, through inspirational poems of their dreams for a better future and of people who have influenced and inspired their lives.

The series is a snapshot of who and what inspires, influences and enthuses young adults of today. It shows an insight into their hopes, dreams and aspirations of the future and displays how their dreams are an escape from the pressures of today's modern life. Young Writers are proud to present this anthology, which is truly inspired and sure to be an inspiration to all who read it.

# Contents

Nicole Cummings  (12)  16
Damien Cliffe  (13)  16
Hamza Sharif  (13)  17
Michelle Moss  (11)  17
Tanjila Begum  (13)  18
Chloe Foy  (11)  18
Charlotte Lapping  (13)  19
Nafisa Sharif  (12)  19
Sara Wright  (12)  20
Antony Simpson  (11)  21
Amy Butterworth  (11)  21
Emily Dunwell  (12)  21
Roy Casserley  (13)  22

## Colne Valley High School

Jamie George  (11)  22
Jason Scott Eastwood  (11)  23
Liam Baker  (11)  23
Alyssa Hollingworth  (11)  24
Fleur Bruszniewski  (12)  24
Luc Baskeyfield-Bride  (11)  25
Jodie Kimmings  (12)  26
Amber Fox  (12)  26
Laura Taylor  (12)  27
Justine Halonka  (12)  27
Terri Rider  (12)  28
Amy Hamilton  (11)  28
Kimberley Hood  (12)  29
Vanessa Lofthouse  (11)  29
Jay Jones  (12)  30
Charlotte Walker  (11)  31
Sam Kershaw  (12)  31
Michaela Lockwood  (12)  32
Kirstie Roebuck  (12)  32
Dannielle Todd  (12)  33
Charlotte Wisely  (12)  33
Jessica Shaw  (11)  34
Amy O'Brien  (12)  34
Ashley Whittle  (11)  35

## John Jamieson School

| | |
|---|---|
| Mark Andrews (15) | 68 |
| Natalie Gardner (15) | 69 |
| Jordan Bottomley (15) | 69 |
| Gavin Rhodes | 69 |
| Luke Hazelgrave (15) | 70 |

## Morley High School

| | |
|---|---|
| Sophie Cook (15) | 70 |
| Catherine Homan (14) | 71 |

## Pudsey Grangefield School

| | |
|---|---|
| Luke Foley (12) | 71 |
| Anya Cross (11) | 72 |
| Amber Carter (12) | 72 |
| Nicholas Wood (11) | 73 |
| Charlotte Hood (11) | 73 |
| Hayleigh Anderson (12) | 74 |
| Amy Edgley (12) | 74 |
| Carl Place (11) | 75 |
| Jack Wilby (11) | 75 |
| Tom Lawrence (12) | 75 |
| Sarah Peel (11) | 76 |
| James Brown (12) | 76 |
| Olivia Hudson (12) | 77 |
| Beth Rothery (11) | 78 |
| Abigail Cook (12) | 79 |
| Rebecca Sissons (11) | 79 |

## Rastrick High School

| | |
|---|---|
| James Carey (12) | 80 |
| Katie Kirby (12) | 81 |
| Natasha Simpson (12) | 82 |
| Charlotte Brooke (12) | 82 |
| Tom Edwards (13) | 83 |
| Alexandra Broadbent (13) | 83 |
| Emma Drennan (13) | 84 |
| Sam Pearson (12) | 84 |
| Adam Johnson (13) | 85 |
| Shoni Gale (13) | 85 |

Liam Bushby  (13)                     113
Erika Leadbeater  (12)                114
Robert Tomlinson  (13)                114
Shabnum Tariq  (12)                   115
Katie Gray  (13)                      116
Lonny Mightly  (13)                   117
Kayleigh Swain  (12)                  118
Sian Watson-Burrows  (12)             119
Katja Johnston  (12)                  120
Abigail Hesling  (13)                 121
Adam Griffin  (12)                    122
Cameron Scrimshaw  (13)               123
Chloe Cordon  (12)                    124
Jaanzeb Khan  (13)                    125
Thomas Bancroft  (12)                 126

## St John Fisher RC High School, Dewsbury
Jack Maguire  (12)                    126
Katherine Lee  (11)                   127
Siân Ginnelly  (11)                   127
Ellie Ewart  (12)                     128
Amy Armitage  (11)                    128
Katie Alderson  (12)                  129
Molly Thornton  (11)                  129
Jamie Abbott  (12)                    129
Aimee Rhodes  (11)                    130
Thomas Hirst  (11)                    130

## Sowerby Bridge High School
Zoey Robins  (12)                     131
Gemma Sunter  (12)                    131
Claire Dyson  (12)                    132
Gareth Poole  (11)                    133
Nosheen Amin  (12)                    134
Olivia Stott  (12)                    134
Tara Slater  (11)                     135
Chloe Ross  (12)                      135
Kerry Firth  (12)                     136
Deanna Stephenson  (12)               136
Sanober Mahmood  (12)                 137

# The Poems

# I Have A Dream

I have a dream
It should be told
The sight of
Beauty, truth and love bold
Love and truth, true love
Faithful, happiness
For evil spreads across
The world
Causing pain and suffering
For does it not affect
Us all, somehow?
I have a dream
It should be told
Not to hide in darkness
Where nothing grows
Shine out bright and
Reach happiness.

**Liam Kubicsek  (12)**
**Buttershaw High School**


# Imagine A Dream

I have a dream that racism stops
I have a dream that crime and violence stop
I have a dream we find a cure for all illnesses
I have a dream there is no hunger

I imagine that drugs are gone
I imagine the world can sing
I imagine all races come together as one
I imagine world peace.

**Luke Terrelonge  (12)**
**Buttershaw High School**

# My Wonderful Dream

Imagine there's no wars
It's hard to believe
No noise or sound
Above is peaceful

Imagine if you are in Heaven
Being a fairy is wonderful dream
Flying in the sky
Touching the beautiful air
Sitting on clouds
Feels like hugging yourself

Imagine there is happiness
Throw the sadness away
Being good is honest
Being bad is cruel

You may think my head is always in the clouds
But I think I should be allowed
To hope for a peaceful world
In which we can all live happily together.

**Khushbu Patel  (12)**
**Buttershaw High School**


# My Little Dream

I have a dream to stop hunger
To feed little mouths with food

In my world no one will starve
And there will be peace on Earth

Stop wars and the food will
Come through to poor people

I have a dream not to be judged
To feed the poor and save the world.

**Bret Green  (12)**
**Buttershaw High School**

# Imagine!

Imagine!
A world with no criticism
No violence, no war

Imagine!
A society with no racism
No prejudice and no class divide

Imagine!
The way it should be
The way you should feel

Imagine!
Walking down the street
And being subject to no objections.

**Kimberly Stones  (16)**
**Buttershaw High School**


# My Dearest Dream

I had a dream that I lived in World War II
We had difficulties of today and tomorrow
Friends help each other and some people have freedom
I wish they could stop stealing
It's not a good thing
We should not throw litter on the floor
The rich people should give money to the poor
And stop bullying forever
And they should have equal money
And everyone should have peace
And violence will end and the doves will fly.

**Umar Nawaz  (11)**
**Buttershaw High School**

## My Dream

I wish I could be a world famous star
And have a super fast car
Give my money to people who need it
So they can have their own footy kit
Buy a box at Man U
And have my nan's home-made stew
Live in a big house with massive bedrooms.

**Liam Tomlinson (11)**
Buttershaw High School

## My Wish

My wish is for the world to be a better place
And maybe it could be safe
And the core can keep its pace
Then we can enjoy our own specific space
My wish, oh how I enjoy my wish.

**Thomas Hatfield-Laird (10)**
Buttershaw High School

## Please

Please can I have some peace and quiet
Please don't start a riot

Please can I have a kite
Please can I have a peaceful night

Please, please buy me a spar
Then I will let you drive my car.

**Matthew Little (12)**
Buttershaw High School

# I Had A Dream

I had a dream that gangs didn't exist
I had a dream there was no shop raiding

I had a dream that people stopped joyriders
I had a dream that people lived happily

I had a dream that there were no racist people
I had a dream that there were no drug takers
I had a dream that everyone learned
I had a dream that everyone listened.

**Bradley Britton  (11)**
**Buttershaw High School**


# My Dream

To be a guitarist in a band
On the stage tall I stand
Excited and happy, feeling the thrill
That's the dream I want to fulfil!

Playing in front of everyone
All headbanging and having fun
For everyone to like us and think we're something new
That's the dream I want to come true!

Music pumping out as loud as can be
Everybody cheering and screaming for me
Touring everywhere from coast to coast
That's the dream I want the most!

To be able to meet all my fave bands
To say, 'Rock on,' and shake their hands
To just be in a band it seems
But this is simply just my *dream!*

**Holly Sheard  (13)**
**Cockburn High School**

# My Dream

I sit in lessons
Bored to tears
I sit and daydream
Forget my fears

I dream of money
I dream of fame
I wish with all my heart
That it wasn't a game

I dream that my dream is real
And not a fake
I sit and dream
Of a wonderful life I could make

But here I am
Still real glum
Daydreaming of what will happen
In years to come.

**Sarah Bateson (13)**
**Cockburn High School**


# My Dream Poem!

I want to . . .

Be a famous actress
Do ballet
Wear Gucci dresses
Be a billionaire

Eat caviar for breakfast
Drink champagne at night
Get ready to party
Party till midnight!

I know what you're thinking
This will never happen to me
But be warned
Just you wait and see!

**Katie Dawson (13)**
**Cockburn High School**

# I Wish!

I wish I could be
A famous dancer
Famous dancer, yeah that's me!

Dance beyond the famous stars
Have my own dancing class
Teaching people who wish to be stars

I'll always be on my feet
Dancing even when I'm in the street

This has always been my dream
To have my own dancing team.

**Samantha Hartley (13)**
**Cockburn High School**


# My Dream!

To be a vet
Operate on people's pets
To help them when they're in need
Or even when they're born give them a feed
To play with them, to nurse them, I'll always be there
I want to be a vet, true and fair
Yes, I want to be a vet, that's me!

**Gemma Skinner (13)**
**Cockburn High School**


# I Have A Dream

I want to be a billionaire
Who becomes the mayor
I would be very happy
Or so you might think
Money doesn't cause happiness
Only world peace will.

**Tom Sampson (13)**
**Cockburn High School**

# I Want!

I want to be a hairdresser
I want to live abroad
I want my own salon
I want to go to college
I want to go to university
I want to drive a car
I want to be the best I can
But most of all
I want to be me!

**Jessica Carver (13)**
**Cockburn High School**


# The Future!

When I grow up I want to be a nurse
So I can understand people's pain so they are safe
I hate the thought of people being sore
It just doesn't seem right
I want to help the poor children
Who are in hospital and need my help.

**Samantha Bentley (13)**
**Cockburn High School**


# Sheriff

I want to be a sheriff
And capture all the outlaws in town
I'll have a shiny badge and a hat that's brown
I will have a big grey horse
That has shiny little shoes
With my great horse only the bad guys will lose.

**Shaun Emmett (13)**
**Cockburn High School**

# Ambitions, Ambitions!

Ambitions, ambitions
What are ambitions?
Ambitions are things you believe in

Ambitions, ambitions
What are my ambitions?
Could I be a singer
Or could I be a star?
Would I be known far and wide?

Ambitions, ambitions
What is my ambition?
My ambition is to be a hairdresser
Why do I want to be a hairdresser?
Oh why . . . oh why?

**Chelsea Conlon  (13)**
**Cockburn High School**


# Ambitions Poem

Could I be an actress
Or could I be a singer?
Ambitions, ambitions
What are my ambitions?

Could I be a nurse
Or could I be a hair-dresser?
Ambitions, ambitions
What are my ambitions?

Could I be a dancer
Or could I be a dentist?
Ambitions, ambitions, ambitions, ambitions
What are my ambitions?

**Kelly Whitehead  (13)**
**Cockburn High School**

# Dreams

Dreams can be good
Dreams can be bad
Dreams can be fun
Dreams can be sad
I lay in bed at night
I dream good dreams
I dream bad dreams
I dream fun dreams
I dream sad dreams
And I dream very, very
Good dreams!

**Natasha Buxton  (12)**
Cockburn High School


# I Have A Dream

I have a dream
A dream to be a star
To be known all over
And to get a fancy car

I have a dream
A dream to be a vet
To help the poor animals
That I have met.

**Megan Geddes  (12)**
Cockburn High School


# I Have A Dream

I want to have a family
One child will do for me
I'd like to have lots of money
By winning the lottery.

**Hassan Ali  (13)**
Cockburn High School

## Ambitions!

I had a cat as my very first pet
My ambition is to be a vet
I got a guinea pig when I started school
My friends thought it was really cool
I've never lived without a pet
Maybe that's why I want to be a vet
If I go to uni I'm going to get a flat
Not to mention a big fat cat
I can't wait in about 8 years
Maybe I'll be celebrating with a couple of beers!

**Amy Lawson  (13)**
**Cockburn High School**


## My Ambition

At first I wanted to be a hairdresser
But I didn't want to handle people's nitty hair
But then I wanted to be a doctor, a nurse or a brain surgeon
Because I'd love to save a life

Then after a long time I was watching TV
And 'The Zoo' was the programme I was watching
So now I want to be a zookeeper
And save a monkey's life.

**Katie Collinson  (13)**
**Cockburn High School**


## All I Want

I want a lot of things, but do I get them? No!
My mum and dad ask what I want for my birthday
And Christmas, so I tell them what I want. I don't get them
All I want for my birthday are some CDs. I don't get them
I ask my parents if they'll get me a phone for Christmas. I don't get it
Their excuse is I don't need them
I know I don't need them, but I want them.

**Rebekah Walker  (13)**
**Cockburn High School**

# My Ambition

My ambition in life is to see the world
Visit Japan
And get my hair curled!

I would go to Peru
Maybe even Holland
To get a clog shoe

My ambition in life is to visit the moon
I know that seems a bit out of space
But I really want to go soon.

**Steven Libers (12)**
Cockburn High School


# My Ambitions!

At first I wanted to be a fireman
Not showing a morsel of fear
Then I changed my mind to a hairdresser
But then I had no idea

One day I sat and thought of what I wanted to be
Then I had one great ambition
And I got it, that's what I ended up being
*A teacher!*

**Jessica Young (12)**
Cockburn High School


# Dancer

D ancing is my passion for everyone to see
A nd I want all the lights to shine down on me
N ow everybody's looking as I take the stage
C ounting down the seconds, turning every page
E veryone is clapping to see my name in lights
R emember all the tears and laughter that happened that night.

**April Haigh (13)**
Cockburn High School

## What Matters

I have a dream
A very big dream
To travel the world
And the seven seas

I have a hope
Without a doubt
To climb a mountain
And hear my echo shout

I have a hope
To be good at art
And draw a picture
With a really big heart

I want all these things
But in the end
I have my family
And my friends.

**Sonya Kumar  (12)**
**Cockburn High School**


## My Future

I'll be a social worker
To help children and families in need
I'll have a big house
Two beautiful cars
My life will be happy indeed
I'll have a handsome husband
And twins, a girl and a boy
I'll dress them in blue
And purple and they'll
Be my pride and joy.

**Shahira Shabir  (12)**
**Cockburn High School**

# Our Leeds Career!

I hope, I hope, I hope
I hope I play for Leeds
With Robbie Hulse
And Robbie Blake
I hope I play for Leeds

One day, one day, one day
One day I'll play for Leeds
I'll be the best player in the world
For the famous football team

We'll make, we'll make, we'll make
We'll make Leeds go to the top
Never lose a game again
And go to the top of the Premiership.

**Ashley Horner & Rajpal Singh Sond  (12)**
**Cockburn High School**


# My Ambition

My ambition is to be
A doctor and a performer
Hard, but very exciting
One minute I'm saving lives
The next making people
Shake their thing
I just hope
The Lord, my God, will
Look down on me
And hear my cry
To be a performer and a doctor
At the same time
How much fun will this girl have
My ambition, my wonderful ambition.

**Angel Muketu  (14)**
**Cockburn High School**

# Life Is Good

Life is full of wonderful things
Sunsets on beaches and big waterfalls
Children playing and laughing together
Oh, isn't life good?

Life is full of wonderful things
Lying in the grass, the breeze through my hair
Adults talking and drinking coffee
Oh, isn't life good?

Life is full of wonderful things
Hilltops full of flowers and the green grass
Teenagers singing happily in the church choir
Oh, isn't life good?

Life is full of wonderful things
Loads of mountains made for climbing
Babies sucking on dummies and gargling away
Oh, isn't life good?

**Jade Nicholson  (12)**
**Cockburn High School**


# My Dream

I dreamt last night
I saw an astounding light
An angel standing there

She spoke to me
And I could see
Her beautiful glistening wings

Then she said, 'Farewell.'
With a jingle of bells
She disappeared into the night

I know this was rare
My memory was bare
Then I smiled and went to sleep.

**Aimee Dale-Barton  (12)**
**Cockburn High School**

# I Have A Dream

I have a dream that someday
No war will there be
No people racist to beings
No one to hurt me

I have a dream that someday
No one will have to lie
No one to tell us we are wrong
No one to tut and sigh

I have a dream that someday
We can look how we like
No one to say we're poor
If we don't wear Nike

I have a dream if someday
It would just come true
Everyone looks different
Because your beauty's inside you

I have a dream that someday
No war will there be
No people racist to beings
No one to hurt me.

**Nicole Cummings  (12)**
**Cockburn High School**


# My Ambition

I am on a mission to
Live out my ambition
To be a footballer
Or maybe grow taller
Whatever reason why
I won't be really shy
Whether it is to be a race car driver
Or a world class mimer
To be in a movie
Or be really groovy.

**Damien Cliffe  (13)**
**Cockburn High School**

# Dreams

Dreams are like beams
Straight in your head winding
Around bed!
Red, blue, black and yellow
You could even meet a new fellow!
You could even sing and
Get a brand new ring
You can go to the beaches
And even eat 20 peaches!
You can even fly or die
A dream is a fantasy
And you can even get
Stung by a bee
On your knee
You can eat the cloud and shout!
Bad dreams are limited
And we wake up
And there's nothing to do!

**Hamza Sharif  (13)**
**Cockburn High School**


# I Have A Dream

I have a dream. A really big dream
But I'm not sure I can tell you
I have a dream. A really big dream
It's really hard to keep in
I have a dream. A really big dream
I'll whisper it to you now
I have a dream. A really big dream
Did you hear it?
I have a dream. A really big dream,
I'll tell it to you louder
I have a dream. A really big dream
I've decided not to tell you
I have a dream.

**Michelle Moss  (11)**
**Cockburn High School**

# What I Want To Be . . .

What I want to be is not simple
Like a buzzing bee
You need a lot of concentration
And definitely loads of education

What I want to be is really sometimes sad
You could even get accused of
Something really bad!

What I want to do is help people
The needle that goes in
Will sooner than later go in the bin

I'm not really into blood
Even though I really should
I'm not really into guts
Forget all the cuts

Although people sometimes act rotten
The mistake you make will never be forgotten
What I want to be is a doctor
Even though it might be a shocker!

**Tanjila Begum  (13)**
Cockburn High School


# I Dream

I dream of being a dolphin
And swimming the ocean wide
I dream of being a dolphin
And coming in and out with the tide

I dream of being a pop star
And singing to the whole UK
I dream of being a pop star
I just can't wait for that day.

**Chloe Foy  (11)**
Cockburn High School

# All I Want

All I want when I grow up
Is to be a millionaire
And to have all the good looks

Acting on the telly
Meeting all the stars
Walking down the carpet
People behind the bars

Asking for my autograph
With a picture took
My face on a T-shirt
With a wink of good luck

I go up for my Oscar
People clapping in the crowd
I look at my mummy
Oh she looks so proud.

Getting in my limo
Waving with my hand
Time to go to the after party
To listen to the band.

**Charlotte Lapping  (13)**
**Cockburn High School**


# Super Mum

I look up to my mum
She is the best
I love her so much
She's better than the rest

She is very nice
She's also sweet
She's all mine
She is the hardest to beat
*Super Mum!*

**Nafisa Sharif  (12)**
**Cockburn High School**

# My Dream!

Wherever you are there's
Always a dream
No matter what it is, but then
One night I had a dream that I was in a stream
It was really weird
But then in the night
I felt a shudder down my back
And that's when I saw a bright light
I ended up in a car
With a bunch of money
I felt really happy and
That's when I noticed a strange pink bunny
I thought it was weird
I felt a tingly feeling inside
I didn't know what it was
And that's when I started to hide
There was a boy, I thought he was really cute
He came with a beautiful flower
He just stood there next to me, telling me to take it
But then he said, 'Now we've got the power.'
I didn't know what he meant
But then he told me I was right
I started to blush
But down the side of my back was a really bad stitch
It started to get dark
I started to wake up, I thought, *that was a great dream*
I was starting to enjoy it
But I noticed it was just a theme
And that was my dream.

**Sara Wright (12)**
**Cockburn High School**

# Dancing

Dancing isn't as easy as you think
But not as hard as on an ice rink
If you do the worm or a jump in the air
You will feel the wind in your hair
But ballet is a harder thing
Feet straight, remember you are the ring
Breakdancing will break you to the bone
So give someone a ring to own
So this is lucky I am a dancer.

**Antony Simpson (11)**
Cockburn High School

# Danny McGuire

I love Danny McGuire
I think he is good
He scores all the tries
And Singfields is his best bud

He always gets injured
But recovers very well
He has his own song
And he doesn't smell!

**Amy Butterworth (11)**
Cockburn High School

# I Wish

I wish I lived in a land of peace
With my beautiful 7-year-old niece
We could have fun all day
And play together
We'd be happy and be friends forever.

**Emily Dunwell (12)**
Cockburn High School

# I Want To Be . . .

I want to be a steam train driver
And my sister wants to be a championship diver

I want to be a cameraman
And they said, 'Yes you can!'

I want to help in a play
Especially in the middle of May.

**Roy Casserley (13)**
Cockburn High School


# I Have A Dream, No More Poverty

I have a dream
For a world with no disease
No poverty in Africa
A cure for AIDS
Clean water

We love hot showers
They only have the river
We have central heating
They only have the sun

We have loving families
Some babies do not!
No laughter
No happiness

Imagine living their life for one day
No hot water
No proper food
Maybe even no parents!

This is my dream
Please follow it.

**Jamie George (11)**
Colne Valley High School

# I Have A Dream

I have a dream
To make lots of money
And live in a world
Where it is sunny

I have a dream
To feed the poor
And not let anyone
Live in the sewer

I have a dream
To change it all
The planet and nature
Let there be no wall

If you think I'm by myself
I think you will be wrong
This is why I wrote this
Poem like a song.

**Jason Scott Eastwood  (11)**
**Colne Valley High School**


# I Have A Dream

S  top the hunger
T  ears of pain
A  frican orphans
R  ivers run dry
V  isions of death
A  IDS runs riot
T  ortured souls
I  gnored, forgotten
O  ver to us
N  ow to make this end.

**Liam Baker  (11)**
**Colne Valley High School**

# I Have A Dream

I have a dream
I wish it would come true
I dream there are no criminals
No pain or misery too

My dream is very peaceful
No stench of crime around
The world will sing in harmony
As crime sinks through the ground

My dream, it sounds quite simple
Yet complicated too
It's where everyone is happy
And no one's feeling blue

But it will never happen
No matter how hard I try
My dream is just for dreamers
Who are searching far too high.

**Alyssa Hollingworth (11)**
Colne Valley High School


# I Have A Dream

I have a dream
That when I'm older
I am going to be a nursery nurse

I'll work with young kids
Feed them and change them
Stop them from crying
And teach them their manners

I will teach them their alphabet
And even their numbers
Tell them what's right
And tell them what's wrong

I have a dream today.

**Fleur Bruszniewski (12)**
Colne Valley High School

# I Have A Dream

I have a dream
A hope for the future
Where the world isn't so mean
And people live as one

I have a dream
A hope for the future
Where there isn't all this fighting
And war is a thing of the past

I have a dream
A hope for the future
Where racism has gone
And prejudice is dead

I have a dream
A hope for the future
Where death is natural
Not the cause of a fight

I have a dream
A hope for the future
Where animals aren't hit
And neither are children

I have a dream
A hope for the future
Where all are happy
With what they've got

I have a dream
A hope for the future
Where stealing has stopped
And greed is no more

But this world is only a dream
Unless we work for it.

**Luc Baskeyfield-Bride  (11)**
**Colne Valley High School**

# I Have A Dream

I have a dream
Just as anyone else
It may not be the same
But I have a dream

To live in a fantasy world
No school, that means no homework
Just fun, real good *fun!*

The beach
The golden sand between your toes
The clear blue sea that's always warm

In this place there is always sun
It never rains
With my friends who are always here to play
Never on my own I have the best time

I have a dream
Just like anyone else
It may not be the same
But as you can see
I have a dream.

**Jodie Kimmings  (12)**
**Colne Valley High School**


# I Have A Dream

I have a dream that
I find out what's at the bottom of the ocean
I have a dream that
I find out where the sky ends
I have a dream that
I can fly to all galaxies
I have a dream that
I can swim to the bottom of the ocean
I have a dream that I
Can visit every country
I have a dream to explore the world!

**Amber Fox  (12)**
**Colne Valley High School**

# I Have A Dream

In February 2006 we went to India
There is so much poverty in India
I wish I could make a difference
So my dream is
That one day I will go back
And help all the poor children
I wish I could make a difference

Also the animals get treated badly
This makes me very mad
I wish I could make a difference
The people treat elephants cruelly
One day I wish I could change this

After my work is done in India
I would love to live in Florida
Where I would own a posh flat
And have a ginger tabby cat

This is a dream
This is a dream
I wish could come true.

**Laura Taylor  (12)**
**Colne Valley High School**


# I Have A Dream

Racism
One word
That never goes away
Who cares?
No one
Black people, white people, yellow people, green people
What does it matter?
I dream we could all be equal
But is that dream just in my head?

**Justine Halonka  (12)**
**Colne Valley High School**

# I Have A Dream

I have a dream for the children , , ,
A dream that they can share
The others that they live with
Will be kind and fair . . .

I have a dream for the children
A dream to go far
A dream with no pollution
No buses, no trains, no cars

I have a dream for the children
A dream that they succeed
A dream with doctors and carers
To help their every need . . .

I have a dream for the children
A dream for their lives fulfilled
The children need to know what we know
So their generation can build.

**Terri Rider (12)**
**Colne Valley High School**


# I Have A Dream

I have a dream for the world
To make it a better place
No more pollution, no more poverty or stealing
Better for the human race

I have a dream for children
To be happy and enjoy their lives
Let them play and learn
Until the day they die.

**Amy Hamilton (11)**
**Colne Valley High School**

# I Have A Dream

I have a dream
Without violence or war
A dream without suffering or hiding behind doors
This dream is where we can all cooperate
And get along like friends
In this dream there isn't, 'That's mine!' and 'You can't play!'
Instead it is, 'We can share!' and 'Yes you can play!'
This dream lets people have rights
So they don't have to fear each other
This dream is where you can care for each other
Rather than just leave them all alone
I have a dream
Without gun violence and bullying
So people and animals can be free
I have a dream
And this dream will hopefully come true in the future.

**Kimberley Hood  (12)**
**Colne Valley High School**


# I Have A Dream

I have a dream
That anyone would dream
Most people's dreams would be to live in Florida
Or New Zealand
But no!
My dream is about life
Everyday life
Bullying, racism and even terrorist attacks
Well my dream would be for world peace
Why can't everyone get along?
No one's different
It's what people say that makes you different
And that's my dream.

**Vanessa Lofthouse  (11)**
**Colne Valley High School**

# I Have A Dream

I have a dream
Of modern society
Living in a world of perpetual peace
If only my dream could come true

My dream is one of many others
Where racism and violence will be no more
Where we can live together beside one another
Why isn't that a law?

My dream is one that could be done so simply,
Where sexism and discrimination aren't common day things,
Where kids wouldn't look at it so mightily,
But instead scowl and throw it away.

As I walk through the school yard I see people on their phones,
Are they playing games or texting?
No, they're looking at any porn they can get their hands on.
How has this world come to be,
Where kids are looking at it so naturally?
How has this discriminating poison got into their minds?

In my dream the world's at one,
There are no such things as refugees,
Because in a world of peace nobody is banished,
We could make this dream a reality, it would be so easy if we try.

I had a dream,
Of modern society,
Living in a world of perpetual peace,
If only my dream could come true.

Oh! When will this world be there?
Please wake me up when we are.

**Jay Jones (12)**
**Colne Valley High School**

# I Have A Dream

I have a dream
Where racism is no more
Peace is a door that is open

Politicians wake to see
That poverty has come to be
It's all over the world as most people know
But maybe Tony Blair can stop it

I have a dream
Where people aren't discriminated against
Because of their eye or skin colour

I know I'm only young
And not well connected
But maybe the people who are
Can think like this
And stop racial discrimination.

**Charlotte Walker  (11)**
**Colne Valley High School**


# I Have A Dream

Maybe it's only my dream or a few other people at Colne Valley's
dream
My dream would be to play in a successful rock band
All of the audience jumping up and down
In front of you, what a great feeling!
All of the manufactured pop blown away
Rock music rocking the day
The feedback and the overdubs bouncing out of the amps
What could be better than a rock band?

**Sam Kershaw  (12)**
**Colne Valley High School**

# I Have A Dream

I have a dream
To be a beautician
To paint people's toes
And to pierce their nose

I have a dream
To be a beautician
To rub off dead skin
And to offer a biscuit from my biscuit tin

I have a dream
To be a beautician
To massage their feet
And to shave their legs with Veet

I have a dream
To be a beautician
Do you think I'd be good?
I do!

**Michaela Lockwood  (12)**
Colne Valley High School


# I Have A Dream

I have a dream that one day I'll become a midwife
I have a dream that one day poverty will become history
I have a dream that all wars will be stopped
I have a dream

I have a dream that nowhere in the world will be poor
I have a dream that people black and white are treated the same
I have a dream that litter is more thought about
I have a dream.

**Kirstie Roebuck  (12)**
Colne Valley High School

# I Have A Dream . . .

I have a dream
A dream where everyone will get along
Never ever get bullied
And sing friendly, happy songs

I have a dream
Where everybody lives in peace
Never any fights
No emergencies for the police

I have a dream
To get a fantastic job
And earn loads of money
So I will not sob.

**Dannielle Todd  (12)**
**Colne Valley High School**


# I Have A Dream

I have a dream with pink hills
Candyfloss mountains
And fudge clouds coming from mills
There would be no more pollution

I have a dream of honey gas
Just a few small changes
Our planet would last
There would be no more pollution.

**Charlotte Wisely  (12)**
**Colne Valley High School**

# I Have A Dream

I have a dream that one day I will become a beautician
Doing people's nails, hair and make-up
Own my own salon
Earn lots of money
But not work all the time
I have a dream that one day I will have children and be married
I hope I will have two children
A boy and a girl
I will be married to a nice, kind man
I have a dream to live until I get old
I will get old and be happy with my husband
In the countryside with trees and flowers.

**Jessica Shaw (11)**
**Colne Valley High School**


# A Vet In Kenya

I close my eyes
And float away
Dreaming I am far away
Elephants, tigers, wildlife galore
A vet in Kenya wouldn't be a bore

Sunsets, calmness and water so clear
No more ivory trading
And no elephants with fear

Lions, giraffes and rhinos
Also wild boar
A vet in Kenya
Is what I'd adore.

**Amy O'Brien (12)**
**Colne Valley High School**

# I Have A Dream

I have a dream
That all the mean people
Will have been and gone
When I get here

I have a dream
That global warming
Is just a warning

I have a dream
Bullying is gone
Forever!

**Ashley Whittle  (11)**
**Colne Valley High School**


# I Have A Dream

There is a girl she is kind of special
She makes me feel warm inside
I'm kind of worried that I will not impress her
The shadow of her body moves around inside my head
In the darkness of the night

I feel no better as I know we can never be
But in this time I love her but she can never love me
I know this because she shows no interest in me
And she has a good relationship with another boy
But she does not know how I feel

I don't know what to do. I feel by myself
I think she might change my world.

**Elliott Dawson  (12)**
**Earlsheaton Technology College**

# I Have A Dream!

I have a dream to change the world
I have a dream to make peace
I have a dream to end all suffering
I have a dream

Do dreams really come true?
Can I change the world?
Can I make peace?
Can I end suffering?
Can I?

What would you do to stop it?
How would you make all peace?
What could you do to end suffering?
Could you or would you have peace?

Why is all this happening?
Who does it happen to?
English?
African?
Asian?
Will the dream really come true
The dream to change the world?

**Claire Lightowler  (14)**
**Earlsheaton Technology College**

# Words To Change The World

Love and peace
Goodwill to men
That is how the world began

Everyone should try and stay
Friends with each other every day
We should all be kind and get along
Hurting others is very wrong

Going out and having fun
All together, all at once
Hitting the town and having a laugh
Looking forward to the future, never the past

No more wars let's all be mates
Let's all go out and celebrate
These are words that change the world
But no one knows what the future holds

Love and peace
Goodwill to men
That is how the world should stand.

**Jenni Webber  (14)**
**Earlsheaton Technology College**

# Stranded For Eternity

There's always a time when you feel lost and confused
There's no one to turn to when your heart's abused
When you've cried so long and your heart's in anguish
You're thinking that your soul will be with those who'll perish
All your cruel memories will linger in your mind
Until you feel the wish to die

What's the point of living a life
When all your deep secrets come back to life?
Those fears and torments that once were true
Have all come back to haunt you
All your hopes crushed, nothing left behind
Energy all drained from soul, body and mind
Suddenly your past begins to rewind . . .

A flashback comes and hits you like a thunderbolt
Your life comes to a sudden halt
All those years shown in front of your eyes
All those torments, hatred and lies
The terrorising moments in which you suffered
Whoever heard your cries and ear-piercing screams
And whoever listened to your nightmares and dreams

With an eye-blinding flash and an enormous whirl
You're back to life and back to the world
Someone appears from the stormed bruised sky
A face full of light and night-black eyes
Your heart fills with warmth and happiness
He says, 'If you are patient, you'll receive paradise.'
He changed your feelings, your heart, your soul
How you thought about your life and world
So my friend take this important piece of advice
And remember something like this could change your *life!*

**Hasifa Naz (13)**
**Jaamla Tul Imaam Muhammed Zakriya School**

# The Inspirer . . .

A boy was born with non-Islamic tradition
Whose father had passed away long before religion
He was a blessing sent from Heaven . . .

At the age of six he had no mother
No sister, neither no brother
He lived like an orphan

He was given to his grandfather
Who did not live for long either
And then to his uncle

He grew up and began to trade
He helped a woman who was needy for his aid
And soon they were married

At the age of forty
He got revelation, which he preached to his wife
With full satisfaction yes, she was the first believer.

Time went by and his wife passed away
Which gave him great difficulty in every way
And so did his uncle

So he suggested he needed a wife
To look after his children and their life
And he married quite a few

He had eleven wives in total
From which ten gave him no children at all
But he still had six from the first

He had returned to his eternal home
With orders of his Lord he had come
To guide us, now he's gone

This person is the best
And distinct from the rest
And he is my inspirer the prophet of Allah . . . the Prophet Muhammed!

**Rieanah Akhtar  (14)**
**Jaamia Tul Imaam Muhammed Zakriya School**

# My Prophet, My Guide, The Messenger Of God

He was born, no father
At the age of six, no mother
Then taken under the wing of his grandfather

He took me from darkness to light and hopefully he will take me
to paradise

He is the one and only beloved to God
Sent down from the skies to all of mankind

He fought many battles, herded many cattle
Completed his mission and proved his commission
He delivered the message far and wide
Yet still he never left it aside
Some refused and called him a traitor
Whilst some obeyed and called him the moderate pain taker

Was it not this prophet who was ever so compassionate and ever
so generous?
He treated everyone equally whether black or white
Was it not him who had mercy on the children and respected
his elders?
What he liked for himself, he liked for others

Is he not the prophet with the sweet tongue who was so tender?
Is he not the proclaimer of truth who spoke no thing but the truth?
Is he not the guide and tutor who taught and spread knowledge
to others?
Is he not so grateful that even when given a grain he was thankful?
Is he not the guiding light who illuminated the world after darkness?
Is he not the prophet deeply fearful of his master that shook and
cried in his prayer?
Is he not the one marked with loyalty who was loved by his family
and friends?
Is he not the supporter of the needy who gave almost
everything freely?
Is he not the ray of light which shone down on this world and
made it bright?

Oh I wish I could be like him
These battles and difficulties he fought
Yet he surpassed them all
His bravery, strength and steadfastness affects me all
Especially his loving and tender manner, which leaves me in
very deep thought . . .

**Safiah Khapi (16)**
Jaamia Tul Imaam Muhammed Zakriya School


# My Teacher

His life was perfect and pure
For all mankind he was a cure
For he was the beloved one
No grief can overcome
For he got hurt and left in pain
That rubbish that was thrown on him was left in strain
Just to spread Islam of faith
Not to look down and for us to stand up straight

He spread and told
That there's one Lord
To bow down and pray
Read his book and obey
To do as many deeds
That we all will need

For he has a beloved heart
That was clean and pure from the start
He knew about Islam and understood
From old age to childhood
He told us about the day of judgement
What to do and what we shouldn't

We can never repay him for what he's done
Now we'll only have to wait for that day to come . . .

**Samiyah Ahmed (12)**
Jaamia Tul Imaam Muhammed Zakriya School

# All Different; All Equal

To establish equality
Was his golden aim
From the harsh deserts of Africa
Martin Luther King came

His favours were so abundant
His deeds graciously done
He was an essence or wise counsel
They called him, 'Tranquillity's son'

He created unity and affection
Between the black and white
He explained about equality between races
Told them to become friends; not fight

Establisher of peace and order
Incessantly striving for justice
Sufficient for his people
Torchbearer of praise and glory

He told us to love each other
For your character, not your race
Judge a person for their personality
Not by the colour of their face

So let us all stand in a circle
Let us cling on tight
Every colour of the rainbow
Not just black and white
*All different; all equal.*

**Afifah Chowdhury (13)**
**Jaamia Tul Imaam Muhammed Zakriya School**

# My Lord . . . My Guide

The bud of a flower crisply blossoming
The petals of a rose slowly revealing
Trunk of a tree, strengthening, towering
Created by the one . . . my Lord . . . my guide

Sun in the sky, rising, setting
Colours up above, continuously changing
Clouds drifting by, filling, releasing
Suspended by the one . . . my Lord . . . my guide

Waves in the sea, crashing, pounding
Foam and the froth, white and spitting
Streams and rivers, gurgling, gushing
Set forth by the one . . . my Lord . . . my guide

Moon is the night, calmly shining
Stars dotted over, winking, twinkling
Planets in their orbit, steadily rotating
Swimming by the one . . . my Lord . . . my guide

Blood from the heart, forever pumping
Lungs in the body, rising, falling
Muscles under skin, contracting, relaxing
All through the one . . . my Lord . . . my guide

Deceased in their graves, calmly resting
People in hospitals, passing, going
My life in the world, slipping, flowing
Back to the one . . . my Lord . . . my guide

Everything I see, from the sky to the sea
Leads me to my Lord who inspires me
To believe all creation, for him is to be
Till the end . . . of . . . time.

**Sadia Qari  (17)**
**Jaamia Tul Imaam Muhammed Zakriya School**

# I Have A Dream . . .

I have a dream that one day I will pass
Even if it's till the breath of my last

I have a dream to overcome, overcome all my fears
Even the ones that no one else dares

I have a dream to please and if so
I'll be down on my knees

I have a dream to stand up and be proud and no
Not anymore be part of the crowd

I have a dream for love and smiles to last as
Long as the river Nile

I have a dream the ball is in my court
So let's play the game of dreams that
Can never be bought . . .

So many haters, so little time
Forget the haters and you'll be just fine

1, 2, 3 here it goes, my game of dreams
To achieve our goals

*Ding, ding, ding* wait by the stream
No one moves unless first a dream . . .

**Fazila Boodi  (18)**
**Jaamia Tul Imaam Muhammed Zakriya School**

# A Blessed Thing

A young girl passed me the other day
Her gaze, on the ground throughout the way
But it was the veil she wore
It showed a sign of modesty for sure

No naughtiness in her walk, nor any pride
I thought I couldn't be like that, even if I tried
But she got me thinking
The veil it seemed like such a blessed thing

After a few months, I gave it a try
And boy, I felt like I could fly
The feeling it gave was incredible
The atmosphere around me seemed wonderful

I realised it wasn't just me
My father would look at me proudly
And my rank was elevated in society
I wasn't the 'little girl' in the neighbourhood anymore
I was a completely different person for sure

Whenever I wore the veil
I felt like I could soar
My heart would burst with happiness
The source of peace and guidance of my life
It was a blessed thing for sure.

**Rukshana Chowdhury (13)**
**Jaamia Tul Imaam Muhammed Zakriya School**

# My Mother!

A dear heart to yearn for
A voice that makes you cry no more
The mind with wisdom that stretches far
She's your shining silver star

The loving arms that curl around you
The care that makes your dreams come true
The one you know that you can trust
The one who shields your heart from rust

She takes you in her arms and sits you on her leg
She tells you not to trouble anyone
Be good, help people, think right and care
And you'll get back more than your share

You'll have friends and you'll have mates
You'll be the one that no one hates
Everyone will be your friend, everyone will be with you
Because you're the one who cares and you're the one who's true

But don't be overjoyful and don't have too much pride
Remember that you've once gossiped and you've once lied
Don't you see, your mother is someone really good!

**Fathima Khatun  (13)**
**Jaamia Tul Imaam Muhammed Zakriya School**

# Turbulence

It was atop the mountainous hillside
As I gazed at the chilly morning sea
It had for long yet been my meditation
The serenity found within that healed

I once used to struggle up this uneven hillside
Stumbling, falling then crumbling into tears
But you merely picked me up and guided me on
Quietening and soothing my fears

I was no on top of the world (or it seemed to me)
My veins were coursing with pleasure and pride
Suddenly the water below roared and lunged
My heart constricted like poison ivy entwined

An eagle overhead cried out loudly
Penetrating my vulnerable heart
Dominance and violence terrified me
Yet little did I realise; it was only the start

Throughout life we encounter meandering roads
Dead ends and rocky paths
Hostile company, stubborn chores
Useless notions and difficult tasks
However all in all you inspired me
You nurtured my mind and led me to think
Although our way is not soft grass and silken smooth
Situations can change in a blink
It's important to face trials and tribulations
With the inner motivation we all tend to hide
As it's the only way we'll reach our goal
The one we ultimately find . . .

**Amina Hajee  (17)**
**Jaamia Tul Imaam Muhammed Zakriya School**

# An Inspirational Feeling . . .

It sprouts within hearts, this feeling so strong
Blinding people from the differentiation of right and wrong
A feeling that glistens in the night
Admiration, a smile, to adore, to delight

The passion conveyed from a mother for her child
For all people and animals, the tame and the wild
The homeless, the blind, the orphans forlorn
Shedding tears for its sake from dusk until dawn

Our leader Prophet Muhammed (peace be upon him) felt this
For his nation, his people, it is he whom we miss
It was embedded in his heart, this affection he showed
For us, to paradise, he enlightened the road

So why is it not existing with us all every day?
We can touch lives, change worlds, with this feeling we convey
Love is my inspiration, for in its path many sacrifices were made
Sacrifices that remain eminent, still, to this very day.

**Syma Alam (13)**
**Jaamia Tul Imaam Muhammed Zakriya School**


# How Could I Forget!

How could I forget . . .
His sleepless nights
And the terrible fights
How could I forget . . .
When blood flowed from his feet
Under the sun's radiant heat
How could I forget . . .
The shedding of his tears
The one who provided comfort for our fears
How could I forget . . .
That he gave me this religion that I have today
And now I want to thank him
He's passed away!

**Anum Naz (15)**
**Jaamia Tul Imaam Muhammed Zakriya School**

# The Divine Guide

Thy name is of faith
It belongs to the believers
And at times mine is at defect
For you were not here to lead us

At times I look upon there from behind a forelock
The colour of the darkest part of the night
Admiring thy resplendent face
Until I find thy sight
And there in the depths of black I remain
Transfixed for seeming eternity
And for a moment I do attain
Complete peace and tranquillity

But even in such alluring places
Inside the depths of imagination
Amongst the most elegant faces
I deem thee God's perfect creation
And to the most high do I turn
In a painful, passionate prayer
For thee do my tears yearn
Be my judgement saviour!

Gold are thy words
With touch of diamond frost
Brilliant and intense views, in which I am lost
Radiant explosions, that penetrate my skin
Elicit powerful emotions, conquering me within

Under the luminous moonlight
The most exalted in his grace
Revealed to me a guide true
In a peaceful celestial place, I perceived you
The prophet, the final, the guide of mankind.

**Raihanah Raja  (16)**
**Jaamia Tul Imaam Muhammed Zakriya School**

# He Inspired Me . . .

He inspired me to care the way he'd give me a cuddle
He inspired me to love the way he showed me his own
I was so happy he was there

He inspired me to play the way he'd set out his toys
He inspired me to share the way he'd give out his things
Even though he wouldn't talk or say

He inspired me to cry the way he'd screw up his eyes
He inspired me to smile the way his lips formed a heart
This is indeed not a lie

He inspired me to learn the way his words were so convincing
He inspired me to teach him the way he carried out his actions
I just wanted him to learn a lot!

His anger is my anger
His laughter is my laughter
His tears are my tears
His last action is my last action
Because this person who taught me is my
*Little brother!*

**Nasrin Begum  (12)**
**Jaamia Tul Imaam Muhammed Zakriya School**

# My Inspirer

Once I was naughty
Oh! How bad was I!
I used to gossip, sing, dance and backbite (and get into trouble
                                                    every night)

Then suddenly, shockingly, out of light a teacher walked into
                                            the classroom

She spoke to me these words
They dawned upon the correct and right
I listened, stared my mouth opened in awe

*She's right,* I thought, *I'll give it a try. It won't work anyway but . . .*
Surprisingly I saw . . .
My life changed in a flash from bad to good it clashed
I started to change very badly to being polite rather than sickly

I respected my elders, helped others, even started paying attention
                                                    in class

All thanks to that teacher who said those words
She had been respected by others and had a very high stature I heard

I see her from time to time, walking steadily or either talking to
                                            another teacher

Then I remember in my mind
It was because of this teacher I changed, because I mimed.

**Hawa Dessai  (13)**
**Jaamia Tul Imaam Muhammed Zakriya School**

# The Brother I Love

I take him as my role model
He is caring, kind and honest
He has a polite way of speaking to everybody
No matter if they are white or black
Or if they are Muslims or non-Muslims
If I am doing wrong then he won't scream and shout at me
But he will speak in his gentle, soft tone
He will always be there for me no matter what
He shares his secrets with me and so do I
He shares his past with me to make sure I don't do anything wrong
He listens to my problems
He cheers me up when I am upset
He is on my side if no one else is
He stops me from little bad doings to make sure they don't
                                          become severe
He encourages people to do what's best for them
His warm comforting smile makes my day
I also pray to God that he accepts his prayers
And may he always keep him smiling
As I love him with all my heart and I always will
This person who I love clearly and really care for is my brother
And may he find happiness and joy for the rest of his life.

**Wajihah Zahid  (15)**
**Jaamia Tul Imaam Muhammed Zakriya School**

# My Beloved Prophet

From darkness he guided me to light
From darkness of knowledge he declared education my right
He taught me to love, be kind and never despair
To speak the truth, be just and fair
His character was the very best
An example he set for all the rest
Instead of leading a life of vanity
He showed me the path of simplicity
To love for my brother what I loved for myself
Even a kind word was charity
He taught me to respect my parents
And to show mercy to the children
To fulfil the rights of everybody
To be good to all animals
To always keep our Creator in mind
For these people he promised reward
Gardens with flowing water, milk and wine

He is my true and real inspiration
My role model who told me who I am
The last and final messenger of God
He is the son of Abdullah and his name Muhammed.

**Kaamilah Sabur  (15)**
**Jaamia Tul Imaam Muhammed Zakriya School**

# The Truthful

T he one who conquered all of the world just for one religion
H e was kind, a good man and saved people even now from the
fire of Hell
E ven on his death bed he cried for his Lord, for his people and
his religion
T he one who'd done good and still to his Lord he would bow
R unning from one place to another without a breath
U niting his religion
T ill his death
H is body be covered in blood
F ulfilling the promise of his Lord
U nusual acts every day sometimes in the sky and sometimes
in the mud
L aughing a bit and crying a lot in his hand a sword.

This is my messenger the prophet pbuh.

**Zahrin Khan (13)**
Jaamia Tul Imaam Muhammed Zakriya School


# A Fascinating Author

Her imagination is so wild
Because of that it makes me smile
Her mind works as fast as lightning
That's why her book is so frightening

How she thought of the school
Was really just so cool

Her interesting, never-ending books
Just make me read on and on
Once I start
I cannot stop.

**Asma Shaikh (15)**
Jaamia Tul Imaam Muhammed Zakriya School

# A Journey To Childhood

As my mind wanders through marshes of memories
It travels back to the time when I was small
An incident still so vivid and clear
A reminiscence that shall never be forgotten

I stood clutching my mother's hand
As tears ran silently down her face
We were looking over the castle battlements
And facing us were 80,000 brave men

My mother pulled out her soft white handkerchief
And all together as one, the soldiers saluted
They were such proud men, so brave and so young
Ready to give their lives for their loved ones

Positioned side by side in gleaming armour
In their unity they emitted a sense of power
I viewed the scene in awed silence
As my heart drew out to these fine, fearless men

So gallant were they, so valorous and valiant
Determined to defend their country as one
My heavy heart wept at the thought of those
Who would lose their lives in their prime and youth

So as I stood clutching my mother's hand
I resolved to be like these indomitable men
So selfless and stout-hearted, so adventurous and tough
Ready to impart their souls just for us

So I too will salute and stand in shining armour
As my mother waves out her silky white handkerchief
Whether I be prince or king after my father
I will be as courageous and as heroic like these men.

**Nafeesa Mistry  (14)**
**Jaamia Tul Imaam Muhammed Zakriya School**

# The Prophet (PBUH)

He was sent to guide us all
So we wouldn't go on the wrong path
Through hardship and pain did he go
For now his religion runs with the flow

As a child he grew
With no parents to love
How grateful can we be
Because we have enough

He was blessed with prophethood
At such an age
With Khadija his wife
He had nothing to be afraid

He fed the poor
And helped the needy
For this was his job
As the Muslim leader

He has inspired me
To be grateful for what we've got
Because the people that don't
Have sacrificed a lot!

He was the last prophet
And may he be blessed
For all he's done
*He was the best!*

**Zainab Ahmed (13)**
**Jaamia Tul Imaam Muhammed Zakriya School**

# Smile!

Hey man! Why don't you smile?
Why don't you smile in a shopping centre walking down the aisle?
Don't look so grumpy or sad
Smile, you won't feel so hurt or bad

To smile it does not cost
Just smile, nothing will be lost
Instead be happy and cheerful, nothing lost
Maybe cheer yourself with a lullaby or a song

Passing people will be more friendly
You'll be treated with respect and more tenderly
No one will get upset about anything
Even the hardest heart from everything

Whenever you're smiling you'll remember anything except for crying
Whether you're selling, standing, laughing or buying
Why don't you smile that pretty smile of yours?
Even on the shortest walk to the longest tour

So buddy! Smile wherever you go
Just smile that big gorgeous smile on that face
Don't be scared, lonely or frightened
And remember you will get nowhere in life if you are grumpy or sad

So now let's smile and be happy and not moody before I finish
And also it takes more muscles to frown than smile, smile my *pals!*

**Khadijah Isap  (13)**
**Jaamia Tul Imaam Muhammed Zakriya School**

# Dedicated To My Mother

There is no woman like her in my heart
That has always played her part
Who has been with me each passing day
To help and guide me through my way

Who knows my sorrows and my fears
And has been there for me through the passing years
Who has taught me the difference between wrong and right
Which leads me to her 'shining light'

She has always been there for me by my side
Looking over me: my guiding light

My love for her I cannot measure
She is my most valuable treasure
My love for her I cannot express
She guides me to my true success

When life seems to be coming to an end
She is always there, to lift it up again

She is always there to encourage
And give her precious advice
Her overflowing wisdom has no bound

My love for her I will always treasure
Her pleasant smile brings me pleasure

Although she may seem apart
There will always be a place for her in my heart.

**Safiya Navsa  (14)**
**Jaamia Tul Imaam Muhammed Zakriya School**

# He Is The Guide

Muhammed, Muhammed he inspired me
He killed no one not even a flea
To the orphans he was a man who cared
With everything he had, he shared
He was a blessing upon the universe
He told us how to read the Quraan
And how to build our imaan
He loved to stay in silence
He was a man full of patience
He'd cry day and night for us,
He would never cause a fuss
All he'd say is (nation) umathy, umathy
Upset or happy he'd give sympathy
Now he's left us and gone
But still he hears our long-lost calls!
We cannot repay him in any way
All we can do it follow his way
To go to paradise we must listen to him
For he was a guide sent down by him (the Creator)
He explained to us our daily routine
He also told us never to be mean
I hope we can act upon this
For this is excellent advice!

**Hafeeza Hussain  (13)**
**Jaamia Tul Imaam Muhammed Zakriya School**

# Reflection Of Faith

Heavy shots in the air
Screaming and crying everywhere
Is there anyone in the world
That has mercy upon them
Like the way our beloved did?
Lifting his hands
After every prayer
Praying for the oppressed ones
It was only he
His unique touch
That reached my heart
And never left
He cried day and night
For the corruption around
He had a lot of patience
And didn't make a sound
Hot stones were pressed
Against his thin chest
But he carried on praying
For he was one of the best
He was left as an orphan
Since his years of childhood
But the strongness of his faith
Was just too good
No one can replace him
For he was sent from above
Oh! How I wish I could express that
Him, I very much love!

**Zakira Khatun (15)**
**Jaamia Tul Imaam Muhammed Zakriya School**

# The Almighty!

He existed from before time
And will carry on existing
On the day of judgement
The good will surely see him

He has no father
Nor a mother
Surely not a sister
Neither a brother

He is totally self-sufficient
And definitely independent
We are in need of him
Not another person

He created the moon and the stars
Don't forget the people in the farms
Nothing happens without his permission
Nothing, not even on Mars

He created the Earth and the skies
He is the truth, not a lie
Everything lives on his command
And on his order everything dies

He sent the prophets to guide us
Not to create a terrible fuss
Those who ignore and don't listen
Then in Hell they shall drink pus

So people of the world, I cry out loud
Believe the almighty
Surely he will free you from Hell.

**Raeesah Bhana  (12)**
**Jaamia Tul Imaam Muhammed Zakriya School**

# Road To Success

A gem amidst stones
A shining stone in the inky black sky
A flower amongst weeds
A beautiful example was she Rabiah Basri

Glorified him with every spoken word
Anticipating the promised reward
In the hereafter where the believer would receive
House under which rivers would flow

Her lips were constantly moving
Her fingers always counting
Tears glinting in her eyes
Employed in the remembrance of her Lord

In her grave she lay
Reproached them as they asked, 'Who is your Lord?'
Do you think I have forgotten my beloved, The Almighty
When I have been buried a mere six feet underground

Her unlimited love astounded me
Her unbounded fear mesmerised me
Her modesty and humbleness is something to which
Nothing can compare

A guiding light was she for the rest of the ummah.

**Athina Zahid  (13)**
**Jaamia Tul Imaam Muhammed Zakriya School**

# The Brave One . . .

The cries of the people
Nearly woke up the dead
As he lay there in the sun
Which burned over his head
He lay there with patience
Tears swimming down his face
As the big rock was brought
And on his chest it was placed
His screams of agony
And the grief and the pain
As the rock was bought heavily
On his bare chest once again
The blood gushed from his chest
But he ignored them completely
For his helper knew the best
His faith was his helper
Never grew weak
'God is one!' he repeated
As his eyes began to leak
After what seemed like a decade
An Arab set him free
For he wouldn't give up faith
And everyone was there to see
The pain that he had felt
Which caused their hearts to melt.

**Salma Begum (14)**
**Jaamia Tul Imaam Muhammed Zakriya School**

# Words Of Wisdom

A time came when I thought I couldn't endure the burdens of
life anymore
With nowhere to go and no one to turn to
I finally sought refuge under a blossoming Magnolia tree
It had been so long since I had experienced any type of happiness
That I almost forgot that the emotion existed
Until I saw a mother hand in hand with her daughter, laughing
All of a sudden I was overcome by overwhelming tears
The tears flowed endlessly, thick and fast
I muffled my cries in fear of people staring, however my large sobs
overtook me
I began to bawl loudly, not caring who saw me or what they
thought of me

Whilst I was engrossed in crying I felt a tap on my shoulder
I spun around to see a little girl no older than four
'Don't cry sister,' she spoke quietly, but with a tone of defiance
'Go away, you've no idea what I've been through,' I screamed
I shot her a look of utter animosity, but instead of walking away
She looked up at me and said, 'My mother, father and twin sister
Have all passed away, I am alone in the world.'
I was ashamed at my behaviour and astounded at her braveness
'I'm sorry,' I whispered.

'My mother's final words are the words that have helped me to live:
After every tear a smile follows. After every smile a tear follows.
Be patient for patience is the key to paradise.'
Fresh tears rolled down my cheeks, not from the pain I bore,
But from the plain sweetness of the words
I wiped the tears from my eyes and looked up only to realise
That the girl had disappeared.

Even up till this day I don't know where she is
Nor do I know anything about her except for the fact that she's
'my little guardian angel'
And somewhere up in the heavens she's looking over me smiling
The girl who taught me how to live with patience
After all patience is the key to paradise . . .

If I can learn to see life in the positive way, so can you.

**Aaisha Esmail (14)**
**Jaamia Tul Imaam Muhammed Zakriya School**

# Uncovered Beauty

I once met an amazing woman
Whose unique characteristics had shocked me . . .

She walked modestly past the attractions of the market
Past the summoning market place she strolled
Heads turned as the graceful figure in black swept past them

She walked, head down, across the road
My gaze fell as she came closer towards me
She raised her eyes towards me and manifested me to accompany her

Hesitation crossed my mind
Silence being our only form of communication
Her glances being the only sign of comfort

She stopped abruptly at a nearby bus stop
Her eyes smiled at me as I stood beside her
'Peace be with you,' she then uttered.

My mouth opened as a few words came stumbling out
As I enquired about her three-piece garment
Her eyes raised to my level, she then began . . .

'This beauty that I have, no stranger has the right to see
Concealed like a pearl is what we should be
This beauty that I have is only a single part of me.'

Her words so true
Her actions so clear
Her characteristics so noble

I once met this amazing woman
Whose characteristics had shocked me
By leaving a single mark of wisdom deep in my heart
She was the one that had inspired me and always will.

**Zainub Kayat (14)**
**Jaamia Tul Imaam Muhammed Zakriya School**

# The Jewel Of Creation

I have been enlightened by the wisdom of his words
He was kind to every animal, every fish, every bird
He was like no other because
He was greeted by every stone with the words of Salaam

His delightful features were more radiant than the moon
His speech was so true - and it would happen so soon
His clothes were as simple as the colour white
And yet it looked as though he was encased in a pearl

He approached a youngster with such tenderness
His smile, his generosity couldn't be any better
He helped the needy, the poor, the orphaned
And he was the most compassionate from all mankind

'Oh my people! Oh my people!' he would constantly repeat
Always prepared to sacrifice his wishes for others
There was not a moment where he would not cry for his brother
And the last words that emerged from his blessed lips were . . .
'Oh my people.'

**Maryam Siddiqui  (14)**
**Jaamia Tul Imaam Muhammed Zakriya School**

# My Hero

I had never heard of anyone like that before
He was so strong and so brave, and had no fear of anyone
He had a mixture of qualities, which would sometimes contradict
each other
He could be fearsome and strong and seem dangerous while at
the same time
He could be kind and gentle as if he would never want to hurt anything
He was compassionate and just and
Even if his enemy was in the right and his friend in the wrong
He would stick up for his enemy
Because he knew that justice was right and it was extremely wrong
to lie

He was loyal and would never turn back
Once he made his mind up
He is my role model and I hope to be like him
I will try to model myself upon him and
Although I know that I could never reach his status
I will try as much as I can to be like him.

**Fatima Mangera  (15)**
**Jaamia Tul Imaam Muhammed Zakriya School**

# My Inspiration

He was brave and bold
With a heart of gold
Feared by the Devil
And respected by the old
Was Hadrat-e-Umar (RA)
His love for Islam
So strong in faith
Like a man with a sharp and silver blade
His love for Akih was forever strong
Bringing people to the right from the wrong
His merciless killer will be avenged
Abu Lulu who was seeking revenge
But die as he did leading the prayer
This stay in paradise will be forever
I pray to the Lord, may he make me like him
As in my heart there is an inspiration within
Of Hadrat-e-Umar of course
Because he is this poem's source.

**Aisha Patel  (15)**
**Jaamia Tul Imaam Muhammed Zakriya School**


# He Was . . .

He was
Caring
Friendly
Funny
Happy
And enthusiastic

He loved
Music
Football
Gaming
Friends and family

He was Stephen Crowe
Our friend.

**Mark Andrews  (15)**
**John Jamieson School**

## Who Inspires Me?

Stephen
He was a happy boy
Silly all the time!
He was good at maths
He loved football
Boccia and other sports
He had lots of friends.

**Natalie Gardner  (15)**
**John Jamieson School**

## Stephen Was . . .

Good at snooker
Making us all try harder
Good at making me pass things
Good at racing me to the lift
Good at saying what he thought
I enjoyed his company.

**Jordan Bottomley  (15)**
**John Jamieson School**

## Who Inspires Me?

Stephen was friendly
Stephen was a good person
Stephen was happy
Stephen always smiled
He was only 15 years old.

**Gavin Rhodes**
**John Jamieson School**

# My Friend Stephen

Thoughtful and confident
A nice person
He made me laugh
He liked sport, snooker, football
Chelsea was his favourite team
He liked the PlayStation
He also liked girls
He made me laugh
When he talked about them
He liked to go to Martin House Hospice
He loved his family and friends

I was proud to be his mate
I'll never forget him.

**Luke Hazelgrave (15)**
**John Jamieson School**


# Friends

Friends are there to help us
Pick us up when we're feeling down
Friends are always understanding
They can lift a heavy frown

If you're hurting and in pain
Upset and feeling sad
Friends are there at all times
To help us through the bad

Not all friends are right beside you
Some are in your heart
You know they are always there for you
Together or apart

A true friend will not leave you
In times of doubt and sorrow
They will be there for you always
Yesterday, today and tomorrow.

**Sophie Cook (15)**
**Morley High School**

# How Dare You Kill Me?

How dare you kill me?
Drowning me in CO2
You have no right to torture me
Soon I shall torture you

Why must you slay me?
Stealing my blood, my oil
Like an oven you cook me
Making my oceans boil

Why slaughter my wildlife?
Why murder my trees?
Why slash them with your knife,
Do with them what you please?

So I will take my vengeance
Upon stupid humanity
Imprison you for your offence
Ruin you for your vanity

How dare you kill me?
There's no more you can do
You had no right to torture me

Now I will torture you!

**Catherine Homan  (14)**
**Morley High School**


# I Have A Dream

I had a dream that there were no wars in the world
I had a dream that there was no pollution in the world
I had a dream that there was no cruelty to animals
I had a dream that poverty changed
I had a dream that there were no bullies in the world.

**Luke Foley  (12)**
**Pudsey Grangefield School**

# A Whole New World!

I have a dream, a dream to change the world
No wars or battles
No depression or unhappiness
This will be a whole new world

There will be no poverty
There will be no hunger
We will be free from evil and sadness
This will be a whole new world

No more pollution
No more extinction
Animals will live and all will be right
This will be a whole new world

Peace and love
Rich and happy
This is our whole new world.

**Anya Cross (11)**
**Pudsey Grangefield School**


# I Have A Dream

I wish that cancer and serious illnesses would die

H ow many people have we lost through murders and lies?
A time when the world was free of hate
V arious people will have to wait!
E veryone stops and wonders

A nd even in rain, lightning and thunder

D own under where Hell is and awful things are too!
R eady or not we're trying to change you
E ven if you are feeling very sad
A smile from a friend will make you feel glad
M ake the most of your life and always be happy!

**Amber Carter (12)**
**Pudsey Grangefield School**

# Have You Ever Had A Dream?

H ave you ever had a dream
O nly one dream to change the
W orld?

T o live forever we want to
O ne chance to live forever

C hange our ways
H ave our lives changed for good
A lways have peace
N obody will die again
G o find your inner peace
E veryone should do it

T hey will have food
H appiness too
E veryone should enjoy the world

W hy do we fight?
O ver such little things
R ivers polluted no more
L ove our lives and
D o what we should to live.

**Nicholas Wood  (11)**
**Pudsey Grangefield School**


# I Have A Dream

I have a dream to change the world
I have a dream to feed people in Africa
I have a dream to stop the war
I have a dream to stop the fighting
I have a dream that there is no racism
I have a dream that the world will be at peace.

**Charlotte Hood  (11)**
**Pudsey Grangefield School**

# Together Day And Night

I have a dream to change the world
For none of us to live alone
For peace and justice, world and life
We'll work together day and night

There'll be no wars
There'll be no strife
Just working together
Day and night

We'll live as one
There'll be a sight
Just being together
Day and night

No more money
No more fright
Just thinking of working together
Day and night.

**Hayleigh Anderson (12)**
**Pudsey Grangefield School**


# I Have A Dream

I had a dream one day that there was no

H atred in people's eyes
A nger in people's hearts
V iolence in people's minds
E nvy you can't control

A ll this should stop!

D ifferences can be made if people just
R ealise what they are doing to the world
E ven the tiny words they say
A re hurting people inside and out
M aybe my dream will come true one day,
          you can help too, who knows?

**Amy Edgley (12)**
**Pudsey Grangefield School**

# Out With The Old And In With The New

I dream of getting rid of the old world, full of murder and neglect
And maybe, just maybe find a new world, full of hope and friendship
A place where people aren't judged by the colour of their skin
But their actions in life

Maybe some day this dream of mine could become a reality
However right now you could help by doing the little things in life
Then in the future my dream really could become a reality.

**Carl Place  (11)**
**Pudsey Grangefield School**


# I Have A Dream

I have a dream about people who are racist against black people
This should not be allowed because black people are the same as us

I wish there were no murders
And the world was very peaceful
Because the world can be a better place.

**Jack Wilby  (11)**
**Pudsey Grangefield School**


# I Have A Dream

I  wish I was famous

H aving a dream is so sweet
A British superstar
V ehicle is top of the range (my vehicle)
E nter the WCC

A s in the World Club Challenge and win

D ream is . . .
R ugby player
E nglish
A nd
M arvellous.

**Tom Lawrence  (12)**
**Pudsey Grangefield School**

# I Have A Dream

I have a dream
A dream to change the world
I have a dream
That people will live in happiness
I have a dream
That people will live without fear

This is my dream
My dream to change the world
This is my dream
To stop all starving in Africa
This is my dream
To stop all the bad and accept all the good

Here is my dream
My dream to change the world
Here is my dream
To get rid of world debt
Here is my dream
For people to listen to my dream.

**Sarah Peel (11)**
**Pudsey Grangefield School**


# I Have A Dream

I have a dream
To make fighting clean
Or to put a full stop to war
Because people are dying such as the poor

I have a dream
That war can stop like a dry stream
Bullets being shot
I want it all to stop

I have a dream
For life to be as nice as a dream
People praying to God wishing please, please, please
So we should act not think.

**James Brown (12)**
**Pudsey Grangefield School**

# I Will Change The World

This world could be nicer
There are some things we could give
To make this world, that needs some help
A better place to live

Treat everyone equally
We should all start to begin
To focus on what's inside
Not the colour of people's skin

Ignore the stupid people
Who are hurtful and unkind
'These bullies are just jealous'
Tell yourself inside

Why have so much war
When we could all have peace?
No war would hopefully mean
That the world's love will increase

There are many people
Who do not have anything
We should all be grateful
And try to do something

We are killing the Earth
With all the things that we create
Let's try and stop it *now!*
Before it is too late!

**Olivia Hudson (12)**
**Pudsey Grangefield School**

# If Only

If only I could stop racism
Stop the sadness and the hurt
Help those people who feel unloved
Feel loved again

If only I could make world peace
Stop the wars and fighting
The violence
And bring love to the world

If only I could stop poverty
Replace the crying with laughter
Make those people who feel empty
Feel full again

If only I could stop global warming
Stop people in their tracks
Make them realise what they are doing to the world
Make them see what is happening!

If only the world was peaceful
Full of happiness and joy
If only we could all be friends
And not argue and fight.

**Beth Rothery (11)**
**Pudsey Grangefield School**

# I Have A Dream

I have a dream to change the world
And make it a better place

I have a dream to end all wars
And see a smile upon their face

I have a dream of a better world
Where everyone is friends

I have a dream of peace all around
And lots of love to send

I have a dream for my dream to come true
Will you share your dream with me and I'll share mine with you?

**Abigail Cook (12)**
**Pudsey Grangefield School**


# I Have A Dream

I have a dream to stop all wars
And make the world agree

I have a dream to make world peace
And let everyone get along

I have a dream to make everyone happy
And get everyone to smile

I have a dream to stop racism
And make religions get along

I have a dream that I wish could come true
So the world can get along!

**Rebecca Sissons (11)**
**Pudsey Grangefield School**

# Of This Sort

Come on, let's pick on him some more
It's not like picking on him is against the law
He's just a weak, little worm
Let's push him to the end; it's the last day of term

Bullying of this sort
Let it not be taught

Look at him, his skin is different
He looks like a dog, he is too reverent
What a pointless pig, he supports a God
He smells of fish, the smelly old cod

Racism of this sort
Let it not be taught

Let's go and smack him, give him a kick
Get him on the floor, let's make him sick
Let's go and threaten him, yes, with a knife!
Let's use these stones, make him take his life

Violence of this sort
Let it not be taught

It's not my fault; he went without a sound
It's not my bullying, why he's underground
Even though I suppose I helped it on a bit
I'll just stay by the grave to think and sit,

Horror of this sort,
Let it not be taught.

I have a dream,
We must work together as a team.

**James Carey (12)**
**Rastrick High School**

# I Have A Dream

In some places
The world is fighting
In some place
The world is worrying

I have a dream
That the world stops fighting
Stop taking sides
And stop all the worrying

People in poverty
Are hungry
People in poverty
Are thirsty

I have a dream
That I give aid
Helping people all over the world

The world is dying
The Arctic
Is melting

I have a dream
I'll stop the fighting
I'll stop the poverty
And stop global warming
Around the world
I have a dream

**Katie Kirby (12)**
**Rastrick High School**

# I Have A Dream

Imagine all the people
Just like you and me
Living all around the world
In perfect harmony

Imagine all the flowers
Fruit and trees and grass
Able to breathe fresh air
Instead of toxic gas

Imagine all the animals
As they were before
The people came and replaced
Their homes with a shopping store

I have a dream
That one day
This will all be true
And we will all live happily
The Earth and me and you.

**Natasha Simpson (12)**
**Rastrick High School**


# I Have A Dream

I have a dream
To keep the world clean
Free from crisp packets
Or broken tennis rackets

Bottles of pop rolling in the wind
When really the rubbish should be binned

Chewed up chewing gum
Stuck on the shoes of people that run

If the world was clean
The beauty would be seen
So put it in a bin
And don't commit a sin!

**Charlotte Brooke (12)**
**Rastrick High School**

# I Have A Dream

I have a dream that could change the world
With a few changes we could all live as one
In harmony, embracing equality
There's no need for us to feel hostility

I have a dream that there was no more violence and war
I wish people did not have to suffer no more
And they did not have to lock the door

I had a dream that there were no guns
And they could just eat some buns
And have lots of fun
And no one gets shot anymore

I had a dream that there were no drugs
And the only people who take them are thugs
It will just bug you
And it will always kill you.

**Tom Edwards (13)**
**Rastrick High School**


# I Have A Dream

I have a dream, it could change the world
It would be so much different to how it seems
No more thugs and no more drugs
No more knives that would be taking lives

Everybody would be the same
No one would be calling names
The world would be a different place
And it would be a happy time for every face

Nelson Mandela and John Lennon
Wanted the world to change into a place like Heaven
The songs that were sung
And the speeches that were made
The world could soon be very much changed.

**Alexandra Broadbent (13)**
**Rastrick High School**

# I Have A Dream

I have a dream that could change
The whole world
A world full of anger and pain
Could change to peace and happiness

If I could change the world
There wouldn't be as much war
We would be all happy
And not break the law

No violence, no drugs
And also no thugs
If it was that no complaints
No one sleeping in lanes

I have a dream that could change
The whole world
A world full of bad
Could change to good

*I have a dream!*

**Emma Drennan  (13)**
Rastrick High School


# I Have A Dream

I have a dream that could change the world
Just a few changes the world could live in peace
People in poverty will decrease, those homeless will have a home
Ill people will be healed
Fateful fights will be stopped
Terrorists defuse their bombs
Wars will not work
Rights will be equal
Ragged racists will be punished
Brutal bullies will be banished
With straight respect for others

**Sam Pearson  (12)**
Rastrick High School

# I Have A Question

I have a question
It's about my dream
Why are homeless so unclean?
Is it because others cannot share
In the money they have to spare?

Why do people bully others
Threatening them with older brothers?
Children cannot sleep at night
Because of all the terrible fright

Why can't all the boys and girls
Live peacefully in the world?
Why do some people have no care
For others that live in a nightmare?

Why do countries have to fight?
Is it just to show off their might?
Why can't we make these wars cease
So we can all live in a world of peace?

I have a question
It's about my dream.

**Adam Johnson  (13)**
**Rastrick High School**


# I Have A Dream

I have a dream that could change the world
We all could be equal, every boy, every girl
I have a dream which is a world without litter
There would be kindness around nobody being bitter
I have a dream there'd be no bullies out there
Everyone would be happy, everything would be fair
So racism is cruel
But respect is cool.

**Shoni Gale  (13)**
**Rastrick High School**

# I Have A Dream

I want to change this world today
There are so many things I can do and say
To change this world to a happy place
To bring together people of every race
Let everybody see
That a massive difference can be made by me
Do you ever see a big bully that's mean to people for who they are?
They hit them, beat them, push them just too far
Me and you can put an end to this
Change this world into a state of bliss
This is my dream
We will work as a team
To make this not just a dream but make it come true
We can be happy and kind to people too
I am going to stop this and make a difference in our lives
You will be happy when next year arrives.

**Narinder Kaur (13)**
**Rastrick High School**


# I Have A Dream

I have a dream of a world with no war
People holding guns to people's heads
And much more

I have a dream to get the world into a better place
But we can't because it is surrounded with jealousy and hate

People's families being touched with a knife
They will never forget that time for their whole life

I have a dream of no racism and no fights
We should all live as one not black versus white

I have a dream that there's no bullies in school
No one walking around like big, hard fools

I have a dream of keeping the world clean
No mean people throwing rubbish in their local stream.

**Fahed Chaudry (12)**
**Rastrick High School**

# I Have A Dream

I have a dream, to make world peace
Because every day the gun crimes increase

Thieves go behind bars, the police don't release
I ask myself, *when will the murders ease up and seize?*

People shoot innocent people from out their car
Their guns be smoking like a Cuban cigar

One thing we need is freedom
People take their own life, then we don't see them

We need to take these homeless kids out of the cold
These poor children have nowhere to sleep or go

When kids get sent to care homes, they don't have a choice to choose
Some parents foster children, go home and abuse them

Imagine how the world will be when it's all back together
Let's make it peaceful till we die, because we will not live forever!

**Moazzam Ayub  (13)**
**Rastrick High School**


# I Have A Dream

I have a dream

Imagine no weapons, no drugs
Imagine no wealth, no thugs
Imagine no guns, no knives
Imagine no one taking lives

Imagine the world together as one
No fighting, no wars, no need for a gun
Imagine no people on the street
No need for the armed British fleet

This is a place were gangsters rule
But really the people know they are fools.

**Alex Simpson  (13)**
**Rastrick High School**

# I Have A Dream

I have a dream
Why is there fighting
When people get hurt?
Why is there killing?
It's such an awful word

Why are there guns?
They are so bad
Why are there drugs?
They make you dopey and sad

Why are there bullies?
They are like a disease
Why are there wars?
Many people are dying without peace

We all want world peace
It makes us all care
Why can't we have no leaders
And just be dreamers

If you're a dreamer
You're going to be absolutely cooler.

**Tabish Ali  (13)**
**Rastrick High School**


# My Dream

I have a dream
That there will be no war
It bugs me, I can't take any more
The sound of a gunfire
The prisoners caught on barbed wire
The screeching of a car tyre
This makes me cry
So answer my question, why?

**Aaron Burnside  (12)**
**Rastrick High School**

# I Have A Dream

Make a wish
Dream it
Abolish it

An argument
Opinionated people
Different views
Different beliefs
No way of compromising
Although the last resort
War is the way they turn

Make a wish
Dream it
Abolish it

A man
A family
A friend
Taken away
With a click of a switch
Finger on the trigger
Gone forever

Make a wish
Dream it
Abolish it

Lives are taken
Innocent lives
Precious lives
Loved lives
All for the sake of others

A better future
That's our dream.

**Lizzie Brook  (13)**
**Rastrick High School**

# I Have A Dream

I have a dream that I can change the world one day
With a few changes we could all live as one
We can live together in a peaceful world

I have a dream that we will all be equal
With no violence or racism
And less pollution for the world
And no smoking on the Earth

I have a dream that we can all help each other
Share wealth and wisdom
I have a dream that the world will recycle

I have a dream that the world will have a dream
To stop everything bad and evil
To turn into a peaceful world.

**Andrew Mead (13)**
**Rastrick High School**


# I Have A Dream

Put your hand on your heart and close your eyes
And I'll show you a world full of scandal and lies
I have a message for all boys and girls
Just stop for one minute and look at the world
Different people with different faces
Different religions and different races
Stand out from the majority
And leave behind your superiority
So many possessions so much greed
Hungry people we need to feed
So open the cages for the white doves
Show me some peace
And show me some
*Love.*

**Olivia Hutchinson (12)**
**Rastrick High School**

# If I Was Given One Chance . . .

If I was given one chance
My dream would become the world
No innocent blood would be spilt
From any violence or crime
No war would be fought
And no tears would be shed

I want my children to grow old
Feeling safe in their world
And have no regrets from their past
I want them to respect their friends
No matter their religion or race
I want them to understand equality
And in return feel no pain

I want all money to be burnt
And all possessions to be shared
All debts to be dropped
And all food to be free
No life is worth wasting
They are all worth saving!

**Louise Swift (13)**
**Rastrick High School**

# My Dream

My dream is that all the world will come together
And every man, woman, boy and girl will grow up
And there'll be no wars and there will be no bombs
Dropping on people's doors

I have a dream that there will be no discrimination
And every race will be welcome in our nation
My dream is that there will be no poverty
And that there will be peace around the world

I have a dream that every boy and girl
Will have a good education
And grow up to help the world.

**Shannon O'Keefe (12)**
**Rastrick High School**

# I Have A Dream

I have a dream that could change the world
With a couple of changes that could make a difference
In equal right and poverty free
The bullies should let their victims be

There should be world peace
And no more wars
Everyone in the world should all be friends
Everyone getting along and setting friendship trends

There should be no poverty
Starving families in poor countries
Nothing to eat and really ill
To give them a home before it kills

There should be no bullying
Beating people is a crime
Pushing, shoving, punching, kicking
Taking lunch money is nicking

I have a dream that one day this will all change
To stop poverty, bullying and to have world peace
It's not a lot to ask
If everyone came together and made it their day to day task.

**Yasmin Williamson (13)**
**Rastrick High School**


# My One Wish

I wish upon a star that no racism
Would ever come so far
The only thing I want is that there will be no illness
So none of my family ever die, and they live as
Long as they don't tell a lie
I wish that there will be no fights, I wish that there will be no war
So everyone can welcome one another
Through their own doors.

**Kulwant Kaur (13)**
**Rastrick High School**

# If I Had One Wish

If I had one wish
I'd change the world a lot
Stop drugs and no one would smoke anymore
What on earth do people do that for?
It harms people's health and sometimes kills
But people say it gives them thrills

I'd help all the poor creatures
But when they're extinct that will teach us
That those poachers did a horrible thing
And we just sat there and did nothing
Animals should be free
To roam about among the trees

I'd stop all violence and war
In my wish they wouldn't exist anymore
It splits up countries from one another
You should treat everyone like a brother
Love them even if they're black or white
Because that's no reason to start a fight

That's all my wish, all those things in one
I wish they would all disappear and be gone.

**Olivia Turner  (13)**
**Rastrick High School**


# I Have A Dream

I have a dream that everyone gets treated the same
I have a dream that no one gets whipped by a cane
I have a dream that there is no drugs
Cannabis, heroin or cocaine
I have a dream that there is no war
Guns, violence or gore
I have a dream of a perfect world
Then we can all work as a team
In peace and in harmony, because this is my dream.

**Chloe Baring  (13)**
**Rastrick High School**

# I Have A Dream

I have a dream
That there will be no wars
Or no innocent blood spilt
For a terrible thing no more!

I have a dream
That bullying will stop
No more pushing or kicking
People should banish the lot!

I have a dream
That there is violence no more
And people live in harmony
As I think it should be the law!

I have a dream
That there is more life
No more walking around
Stabbing others with knife!

I have a dream
That others will share
No more terrible greed
And others will care

I have a dream
That there will be world peace
Everyone sharing and caring
For my nephew and niece
I have a dream
That my dreams will come true
Especially this one
And I think you would too.

**Rebecca Fletcher (13)**
**Rastrick High School**

# I Have A Dream

I have a dream
For there to be no wars
For people to live
And stop dying in fours

I have a dream
For there to be life
And to stop the people
From being killed by a knife

I have a dream
For there to be no death
To help the people
Stop uttering their last breath

I have a dream
For there to be no blood
Spilt for no reason
To leak into the mud

I have a dream
For there to be no kidding
And I think most people
Would be more than willing

I have a dream
For there to be more trust
To keep the people
From biting the dust

I have a dream
For there to be no fear
To stop that awful scent
Of death coming so near

I have a dream
For my dream to come true.

**Thomas Dyson  (13)**
**Rastrick High School**

# I Have A Dream

I have a dream that could change the world
With a few changes we could all live as one
I have the chance to do all
That racism should be stopped all around the world
That we should share wealth in equal rights
And that we should have world peace in our eyes
It doesn't matter what you look like
In everyone's eyes, you will be seen equal
One day all blacks and whites will be holding hands
And even maybe sharing lands!
I have a dream that one day the entire world will be sharing wealth
Money won't be a problem, children will have
A good education and have good health
Wars will be stopped one day
And no one will have to pay!
Hopefully, granted there will be world peace

And so we will live in world peace
Happy and joyfully we won't be seized.

**Maryam Saeed (12)**
**Rastrick High School**


# I Have A Dream

I have a dream, that could change the world
That everyone will listen to the story's end

I have a dream, that involves the youth
No more lies, just tell the truth
I have a dream, that dream is strong
It will last forever it won't be long

I have a dream, that won't go away
If we all work together we can do it today

I have a dream, that I'm sharing with you
Do what I did, it's up to you

I have a dream.

**James Storry (13)**
**Rastrick High School**

# I Have A Dream

I have a dream
That one day they will find a cure for cancer
So no one will ever die of it again

I have a dream
That one day there will be no poverty
And all the people will survive

I have a dream
That one day people will stop hurting each other
And live in peace

I have a dream
That one day there will be no wars and the
Whole world will be friends

I have a dream.

**Ben Thornton  (13)**
**Rastrick High School**


# I Have A Dream!

I have a dream that could change the world
With a few changes we could live as one
Imagine no sexism, no racism and no killing
Some people say it would be quite thrilling

In harmony, embracing equality
There's no need for us to feel hostility
I have a dream of no religion too
No terrorist to make us feel blue
I have a dream of no war
No more blood and no more gore
Imagine being together
Black and white forever.

**Abigail Malbon  (12)**
**Rastrick High School**

# I Wish

I wish that we could change the world
With a few changes we could all live as one
In harmony, embracing equality
There's no need for us to feel hostility

We don't want war
Not anymore
Innocent blood spilling
Is unwanted like a child crying

No drugs
Or thugs
No smoking
We don't want any choking

Diseases, no one wants them
Like eating a flower's stem
Everyone is equal
But it doesn't fit together like a sequel.

**Thomas Ambler (13)**
**Rastrick High School**


# I Have A Dream

I have a dream
That the world will gleam
There would be no war
At your front door
We would all have rights
No need to have fights
There would be world peace
Even in Greece
There would be no bad bugs
Or bad drugs
So let me just say
Peace every day.

**Linzi Townend (12)**
**Rastrick High School**

# I Have A Dream

I have a dream that could change the world;
People would never be the same
Life would change from being one unlucky game
Slowly but surely I would make a difference

I would stop all violence and war
Anything harmful would be no more
Slowly but surely I would make a difference

Equal rights no matter sex, religion or race
You wouldn't be judged by the colour of your face
Slowly but surely I would make a difference

There would be no killing animals for their fur, skin or meat
The entire world would be tidy and neat
Slowly but surely I would make a difference

No harming children because they don't understand
We would all work together hand in hand
Slowly but surely I would make a difference.

**Hayley Plummer  (13)**
**Rastrick High School**


# I Have A Dream

I  have a dream of

H appiness and peace
A ll work together
V ery happy forever!
E ach other

A s one

D oesn't matter about the weather
R ethink what you do
E nd evil
A nd be yourself, just as you are
M y perfect world!

**Charlotte Hickey  (12)**
**Rastrick High School**

# I Have A Dream

I have a dream
Everyone is one team
People have a theme
I wish everyone would get along
Like cream

Why can't we join each other
And be like sister and brother
Get along with each other
And all work as a team

It doesn't matter if you're black or white
If we come together we can get along alright
Does anyone care?

We are like the weather on and off
So people get along as one
Now end all this evil
Live life to the full

We are all the same
But have different names
These are really board games
This is all pain.

**Georgina Oliver** **(13)**
**Rastrick High School**


# Imagine

I have a dream
M y imaginary world
A ll we need is harmony
G uns and rifles shooting people
I n this world
N o one caring for one another
E veryone, let's work in a team.

**Saffa Hussain** **(13)**
**Rastrick High School**

# I Have A Dream

If we were to change the world
I'd hope there wasn't any money
There'd be no one robbing banks
And thinking it was funny

There wouldn't be any borders
No names or possessions
The world wouldn't be in different corners
The world would be together

Our world would be a peaceful place
Full of life and kindness
If people stopped all this hate
The world would be harmless

There wouldn't be any discrimination
No bullying or racism
The Earth has a big population
But we'll learn to live together.

**Daniel Walker  (12)**
**Rastrick High School**


# I Have A Dream

I have a dream that could change time
With a shining sun
Some whining bees
Water dripping beneath the trees
A little rainbow sprouting from the clouds
Forests and owls hooting aloud

Racism is not the answer
But a bulging binding band
Can stop it all

People say that they're bullies
But all they are is pathetic
Woolly wussies!

**Elliott Stoutt  (13)**
**Rastrick High School**

# I Have A Dream

If I had a chance to change the world
This is what I'd change:
Bullying and racism
The way people behave
There would be no religions
And nothing to believe
Everyone would be happy
And everyone would see

That in this world right now
We are a world of need
We are a world of fighting
And everyone is in need
No hatred and no jealousy
In my ideal world
There would be no possessions
Everyone would own the world . . .

No one would be rich
No one would be poor
No one would have less
No one would have more
No one would be stupid
No one would be clever
Everyone would love each other
Whatever the weather!

**Rosie O'Hare (13)**
**Rastrick High School**

# I Have A Dream

I have a dream
One that can change our lives
And everybody will be happy
When next year arrives
I dream we're all reunited
Together we'll be one
Together we can live our lives
Laughing from dusk till dawn
Not a tear dropping
Not one sad face
Everybody joining together
People from every race
Think about it
Everybody side by side
Everybody holding hands
Nobody has to hide
No more bullies
No more fights
No more racism
Because everybody's got the same rights
We can make a difference
If we all just try
So open your hearts
And make the world a blueberry pie.

**Anouk de Bokx (12)**
**Rastrick High School**

# I Have A Dream

I have a dream of a free world
No racism or discrimination
No fighting in this world of peace
All throughout the nation

I have a dream of a clean world
No sign of litter anywhere
To not see cleaners cleaning up
Maybe you'd be more aware

I have a dream of a good world
No stealing or breaking windows
No robberies at an Underground station
No fighting any evil foes

I have a dream of all these things
Right to the end of time
Making people feel a lot better
At the end of my rhyme.

**Ben Maffin (12)**
**Rastrick High School**


# I Have A Dream

I  have a dream that there will be no perverts

H  elp people that need help
A  nd the world will be a better place
V  ery good people like me and you
E  ventually this will become true

A  ny day, some day

D  ream a big dream
R  ead it out loud
E  very day a bit will come true
A  nd tell everyone
M  y dream will one day come true.

**Jake Higginson (13)**
**Rastrick High School**

# I Have A Dream!

Visualise a world with freedom from war
Visualise a world with no rich or poor

Visualise a world all becoming one
Visualise a world with all hatred gone

Visualise a world with a cure for disease
Visualise a world with everyone at ease

Visualise a world with happiness all round
Visualise a world with no poverty found

Visualise a world with no violence or racism
Visualise a world without any favouritism

Visualise a world where everyone's tame
Visualise a world with no fear or pain

Visualise a world with no abuse or crime
Visualise a world that lasts a lifetime

Visualise a world with your imagination
Now make our world your creation!

**Lindsay Hirst  (13)**
**Rastrick High School**


# I Have A Dream

I  n this life we must pull together

H  armony, peace, love forever
A  ll we hear is animosity
V  ery scary, why me?
E  veryone living in unity

A  nd no more animosity

D  eath long gone, life to live
R  eal fun and laughs with
E  vil people gone away
A  nd happiness to stay
M  y dream is this way!

**Matthew Jaggar  (13)**
**Rastrick High School**

# I Have A Dream!

Picture a world in which no one is poor
Everyone is equal
No one is greedy for more
Everyone shares
No one is penniless or in need
For success you only need
Brains to succeed!

Picture a world where everyone is united
Working together
No need for fighting
Everyone in agreement
Treating each other the same
Listening to each other's views
No one to blame!

Picture a world of laughter and fun
Respecting each other
Uniting as one
To conquer all evil
To conquer all fears
So friendship and joy replaces
The tears!

Picture a world which you like to live in
Set yourself a challenge
Close your eyes, imagine
Visualise a world of happiness and love

Now open your eyes
See the sign of a dove!

**Elinor Thomas  (13)**
**Rastrick High School**

# I Have A Dream

A child dislikes school
So boring and stern
A child dislikes school
Always having to learn
A child prefers home
So peaceful and free
So why, do I ask
Do the fists close on me?

A child shares a joke
With their parents I'm sure
A child shares a joke
When I'm seeking a cure
For my bruises and cuts
From my head to my feet
My parents are harsh
It is me that they beat!

A child is so happy
While I sit in fear
A child is so happy
While I shed a tear
A child only cries
Not often, so rare
A child only cries
For their lost teddy bear!

My parents are hard
And so angry they seem
For life to be happy
For me that's *my dream!*

**Bethany Mcardle  (13)**
**Rastrick High School**

# I Have A Dream!

I have a dream to change the world
One I want everyone to hear
I hope one day my dream will come true
True for me and true for you!

People cower down in fear
It shouldn't be like that
Cowering and just because
All the trouble people cause

I have a dream to change the world
One I want everyone to hear
I hope one day my dream will come true
True for me and true for you!

Racism, sexism, it's all the same
I have a dream that it will all go away
Why is there need for all of this stuff
Like gangsters all acting tough?

I have a dream to change the world
One I want everyone to hear
I hope one day my dream will come true
True for me and true for you!

**Amy Barnfather  (13)**
**Rastrick High School**

# I Have A Dream

When will we allow peace
To flow around this world?

Imagine a place
Where there's happiness and grace

Imagine a place
Where there's harmony with each other

Imagine a place
Where there's no discrimination

Imagine a place
Where there's peace and no war

Imagine a place
Totally racism-free

Imagine a place
Where there's unity, equality and no superiority

Imagine a place
Where we unite as one

Imagine a place
Where there's no poverty

Imagine a place
Where there's a perfect race

Will my dreams come true?

**Kamari Kennerdale (12)**
**Rastrick High School**

# I Have A Dream

I have a dream
To make the world
A better place

I have a dream
To stop all the
Violence in the world

I have a dream
To ban all drugs
To stop the bad

I have a dream
To make hate
Into love

I have a dream
To make sadness
Into happiness
*I have a dream!*

**Lucy Stoker  (12)**
**Rastrick High School**

# If I Had One Wish!

If I had one wish
To change the world
People wouldn't be foolish
Like every boy and girl

If I had one wish we'd all be as one
No racism, no bullying
And nobody would be alone!

There'd be no black, no white
And definitely no wars
We'd all get along
Even behind closed doors

If I had one wish
Smoking would be banned
The air would be clear
And you'd save about a grand!

If I had one wish
To change the world
We'd all make friends
And make a broken heart mend!

**Jemma Walker  (13)**
**Rastrick High School**

# Selfish Dreams

Dreaming is an ambition
A subconscious goal
An exciting superstition
The meaning of the soul

A world without war
Would be a thing of beauty
A huge doorway
Understanding everyone's duty

I have a dream
Of a perfect world
Where we all work as a team
Like a united planet

But some of my dreams
Are completely selfish
It's like balancing beams
To read my wish.

**Oliver Smith  (12)**
**Rastrick High School**

# I Have A Dream

The Earth is like Hell
And we're the little helpers
Working for the Devil
Why racism? Why cruelty?
Oh why do men go into war and die?

And if you want world peace
You've got to sort out the
War in the streets

Water turns to blood
Love turns to hate
It's time we think
About what's bad and what's good
For God's sake

Why can't we just be free?
Oh I cry, oh I plea
We need to be happy
That's what I see.

**Liam Bushby (13)**
**Rastrick High School**

# I Have A Dream

I'd like to live in a peaceful place
Where people aren't judged by the look of their face

With a few changes we could live as one
Where there is no such thing as trickery or cons

Maybe you could share this vision with me
Open your eyes and imagine and after a while you'll see

Racism-free and fair-trade land
Is definitely what I've planned

If we could live in a world which we all share
If someone said something nasty other people would care

Rainbows and pollution-free clouds would be quite nice
A big chocolate cake, well maybe just a slice

Peace and karma is where I want to be
That door is closed but only you have the key.

**Erika Leadbeater (12)**
**Rastrick High School**


# I Have A Dream

I have a dream
That could change the world
With a few changes we could all live as one
In harmony, embracing equality
There's no need for us to feel hostility

The world is like a round ball
Always moving with little people
And animals inside
People moving always moving and
Talking like a mouth of a blue whale
Whales are big, bigger than anything
You have ever seen, like the whale
Crashing onto the beach and making
A disaster happen.

**Robert Tomlinson (13)**
**Rastrick High School**

# I Have A Dream

Aspire to a world where peace is in our hearts
Aspire to a place where black and whites aren't apart
Aspire to a world where poverty and prejudice is banned
Aspire to a place where everyone holds hands
Aspire to a world where unity can stand its ground
Aspire to a place where bullying isn't found

Imagine it today
Visualise it tomorrow

Aspire to a world where there's freedom of speech
Aspire to a place where poor children are reached
Aspire to a world where crime is too old
Aspire to a place where slaves aren't sold
Aspire to a world where equality is everywhere you go
Aspire to a place where racism is a foe

Imagine it today
Visualise it tomorrow

Aspire to a world where violence is put to a stop
Aspire to a place where freedom is at the top
Aspire to a world where abuse is taken away
Aspire to a place where fear can't get to us in any way
Aspire to a world where no war's taken place
Aspire to a place where there's happiness and grace

Imagine it today
Visualise it tomorrow

Aspire to a world where everyone can be right
Aspire to a place where we are all bright
Aspire to a world where the white dove flies
Aspire to a place where the blind can see the skies

Imagine it today
Visualise it tomorrow.

**Shabnum Tariq  (12)**
**Rastrick High School**

# I Have A Dream

I have a dream that no one will starve
Love and unity into this world we'll carve
No one will be poor and needy,
No possessions, so we can't be greedy
It's the sweetest song you'll ever hear
There's no more hate and no more fear
No children crying in the night
Hope is rising like a kite
No people living in a ditch
No one poor and no one rich
No one evil and no one sly
No bullies that will make you cry
No one commits suicide
Because we're standing side by side
No religion, no countries and no war
And we'll be happy for evermore
We just need to remember one thing
We're all equal and the happiness we will bring.

**Katie Gray  (13)**
**Rastrick High School**

# I Have A Dream

If there were no killers
The world would be ace
Not running from them at such pace!

If the world just settled down
People wouldn't walk with a frown
If people didn't get judged by the colour of their skin
Making them feel like they're living in a bin!

I have a dream that there would be no war
No stabbing or shooting anymore
Making other people's bodies sore
We don't need this gore

Everything should come to a halt
With the speed of a lightning bolt
Too many people are dying by the gun
But the killers just think it's lots of fun.

**Lonny Mightly (13)**
**Rastrick High School**

# I Have A Dream

*Envision a world*
Where everyone is equal

Envision a world
Where colour doesn't matter

Envision a world
Where people stand up

Envision a world
Where people speak up

Envision a world
Where people listen

Envision a world
Where mankind walk the same street

Envision a world
Where men stand in unity

Envision a world
Where peace rings

Envision a world
Where harmony is heard

Envision a world
Where the white dove flies

Envision the world in perfect bliss
*Can you imagine a world like this?*

**Kayleigh Swain  (12)**
**Rastrick High School**

# I Have A Dream!

What if everyone was the same
Instead of playing this awful game
I have had a dream
That we're all on the same team

All the discrimination
All work as one nation
Why can't it be a better place
Instead of it being a disgrace?

If we all work together
We will live forever
Why not join each other
And be like sister and brother

I   have a dream

H  appy and nice
A  nd sweet and peaceful
V  ery good people like you and me
E  xtremely brilliant world

A  nd a happy one too

D  ream big dreams
R  ead all about them
E  scalate to adventure
A  nd tell the world
M  y dream!

**Sian Watson-Burrows  (12)**
**Rastrick High School**

# Harmony

Peace in the world
Bliss with each other
Harmony!

The world should be safe
No worries at all
Harmony!

Equality to all
Plus the freedom of speech
Harmony!

Stop poverty and racism
Forever and for now
Harmony!

This is a world that I imagine
It will become so if you can help me

Make this world tomorrow!
Harmony!

**Katja Johnston  (12)**
**Rastrick High School**

# I Have A Dream

Have you ever wondered why a man walks down the road in fear?
The answer my friend is that he is afraid
Afraid of his breed
His creed
His origins
No man should have to feel like that
It must stop

Do you ever ask yourself why that woman has got broken
Bones and bruises?
The answer my friend is that she has been raped
Stripped of her pride
Her dignity
No woman should have to go through that
It must stop

Ask yourself, why are those people dying of starvation?
The answer my friend is that some countries don't have any food
While others have too much
It must stop

Our lives are like a red rag to a bull
You can make my dreams become reality.

**Abigail Hesling  (13)**
**Rastrick High School**

# I Have A Dream

Everyone has a dream
But I'm going to show mine in a rhyming scheme
I think there should be peace
This world shouldn't need police

Racism must come to a halt
This world has a major fault
Terrorism must end
They want the law to bend

Everything must stop!
Little kids rob in the shop
The world is getting bad!
It's making people mad!

You have a choice to change this world herein
People being picked on because they're fat or thin
There's no point in hate
People are dying at a fast rate.

**Adam Griffin  (12)**
**Rastrick High School**

# I Have A Dream

I have a dream that could change the world
With a few changed we could all live as one
In harmony, embracing equality
There's no need for us to feel hostility

Imagine no *racism*
Both colours together
Black and white together
Both groups will be there forever!

Imagine world peace
No fighting, no killing and no slaves anywhere
How can you be a slave
Working yourself to an early grave?

How about no litter?
The world would be a better place
If there was no litter
The world wouldn't be so bitter.

**Cameron Scrimshaw  (13)**
**Rastrick High School**

# I Have A Dream

One who tantalises, torments, teases and oppresses
Beats, intimidates, harms and upsets
No bullying equals happiness

One who is biased, sexist, racist or discriminatory
Who notices the difference between big and small,
Male and female, black and white
No discrimination equals happiness

One who is equal, a match or as good as another
On the same level or the same on both sides
Equality equals happiness

One who is poor, has a lack, rarity or scarcity
Without food, water or a loving home
No poverty equals happiness

One who is united, linked, connected or in unison
A group of people regarded as one
Unity equals happiness

One who is free of bullying, discrimination or poverty
Who lives in a world of unity, equality and peace
This is a happy person
And this is my dream.

**Chloe Cordon (12)**
**Rastrick High School**

## I Have A Dream

I have a dream
To become a choreographer
To teach others
If only that was me!

I believe that everyone can do something
Everyone has a talent
If only I could point them in the right direction
If only that was me!

I have a dream
That they may look up to me
As I look up to my teacher
If only it came true!

**Katherine Lee  (11)**
**St John Fisher RC High School, Dewsbury**


## My Dream

I have a dream . . .
To become something great

I have a dream . . .
To not be afraid

I have a dream . . .
To stop bullying

I have a dream . . .
To stop racism

I have a dream . . .
For everyone to be happy

I have a dream . . .
For peace.

**Siân Ginnelly  (11)**
**St John Fisher RC High School, Dewsbury**

# I Have A Dream

I have a dream . . .
That one day everybody will get along
So that everybody will have a peaceful life

I have a dream . . .
That there will be no more poverty and there
Will be less people
Dying of starvation and hunger

I have a dream . . .
That there is no pollution
And the air is clear

I have a dream . . .
That one day
I will be a double Olympic champion
Like Kelly Holmes

I have a dream . . .
That this year England
Will win the World Cup

**Ellie Ewart (12)**
**St John Fisher RC High School, Dewsbury**


# I Have A Dream

I have a dream that the world makes peace
No more poverty
No more wars
No more fights
No more hatred
No more pollution
No more hurricanes
To build my own orphanage
To help the homeless
To make equal rights
No more Third World.

**Amy Armitage (11)**
**St John Fisher RC High School, Dewsbury**

# I Have A Dream

I have a dream. One world, one rainbow, one family!
The children's lives will be as carefree as an ice cream
Sprinkled with hundreds and thousands
Where death is like a magical mystery tour, like a never-ending nap
And unknown to men
Where jobs aren't a big heavy sack burying you into the floor
Where living is like a song or dance
Enjoyable with ups and downs where everyone joins in together
Where different nationalities blend together like
Paint on an artist's pallet
I have a dream. One world, one rainbow, one family!

**Katie Alderson  (12)**
**St John Fisher RC High School, Dewsbury**


# I Have A Dream

I have a dream to sing a song and everyone stops and listens,
I have a dream to help people in the Third World by living like them,
I have a dream to speak out as one,
I have a dream to build my own orphanage to look after children,
I have a dream to look after abandoned pets,
I have a dream to create my own medal and call it the 'Dove of Peace',
I have a dream to make a never-ending cake so no one is ever hungry.

**Molly Thornton  (11)**
**St John Fisher RC High School, Dewsbury**


# My Dream Is . . .

World peace
Equality of the races
A figure head in the future
Religions forming world unity
The concept of war a dormant thought.

**Jamie Abbott  (12)**
**St John Fisher RC High School, Dewsbury**

# I Have A Dream

I have a dream of a world with no war
I have a dream of a world with no hate
Like a fire no longer burning
I have a dream of a world with no anger
Like no bricks falling
I have a dream of a world without poverty
I have a dream of a world with no disease
Like no leaves falling from a tree
I have a dream of a world with no sadness
Like a flower not drooping
I have a dream of a world full of joy
I have a dream of a world where everybody is friends
Like an on-going party
I have a dream of a world without riots
I have a dream of a world without death
I have a dream of a world without pain and suffering
Like no walls crashing down on top of you.

**Aimee Rhodes (11)**
St John Fisher RC High School, Dewsbury


## I Have A Dream

All races living in harmony together
I dream of all children playing together
I dream of people of all races sharing food
I dream of everyone being treated with respect
I dream of everyone having the same rights
I dream of no one being cruel
I dream of a perfect place
A place of peace.

**Thomas Hirst (11)**
St John Fisher RC High School, Dewsbury

# The World As A Different Place

I have a dream
Of a perfect Earth
Where children can play
And not get hurt

The sky would be blue
And roses would grow
A safe environment
Where the sun would glow

Summer would stay all year long
No rain, snow or thunderstorms
Just peace on Earth
As a beautiful day dawns

Do you agree?
Do you dream this too?
Do you want the world to be this way?
Maybe if only God knew.

**Zoey Robins (12)**
**Sowerby Bridge High School**


# My Dream

I wish it could be summer every day
With the creamy ice cream melting over my fingers
I wish I could go to the beach every day
With the glistening sun reflecting off the sparkling sea

I wish there could be a cure for diseases
So that everyone could lead a happy life
I wish that poverty would end
And that everyone who is homeless has a home

I wish people who live in poor countries
Could get more money so they can afford food.

**Gemma Sunter (12)**
**Sowerby Bridge High School**

# Think About Your Dreams!

Think about
Finding a better cure for horrible
Horrific cancer
Making you cry
Pain
Thinking of the time
How long
Tick-tock, it's passing

Think about
Finding a better medicine for
Painful cancer
Sickly
Painful cancer

Think about
All the little, cute, hurt children
Having a chance
No more pain
No more hunger
More life

Think about living in happiness
No more racism
No more prejudice
One day maybe, just maybe,
My wishes may come true.

**Claire Dyson (12)**
**Sowerby Bridge High School**

# A Dream Come True

This is a dream
A dream to come true
I am sat in the changing room at Twickenham about to
Go on to England's rugby pitch
This is a moment never to forget
Then I get chosen for the team
We run on to the pitch
We all line up to sing the National Anthem
I look up to see my mum crying with joy
My dad looks proud enough to cry himself
Then it's the kick off
The whistle goes to signify kick off
I catch the ball, I am petrified
I run as fast as I can
All I can hear is the crowd cheering me on
My heart is pounding like a speaker
I see the opposition running at me like a herd of rhinos
Then I pass
I don't know what is going to happen
Then we score
I leap with joy and shout
'We've scored!'
The game is over, we've won!
Then the World Cup is presented to me
Then I pass the trophy down the line
Then I wake up, it is Sunday morning so I get changed
To go play rugby for my team Halifax RUFC
I smile as I am chosen for the team
No anthem this time but Mum and Dad still proud
Some day my dream *will* come true!

**Gareth Poole  (11)**
**Sowerby Bridge High School**

# My Personal Dream

I wish people will become nice to each other
That all the people will accept each other no matter what colour they
are
I have a dream that people will stop drugs and smoking
And that everyone will not kill and be violent
As well as that all the bad people will become good
I wish that everyone lives for an extended life
I have a dream that the world will only contain peace
Also I have a dream that there shall be no difference between wealthy
And unfortunate people
That this world is the cleanest
I have a dream that no wars even take place
I wish that all the hatred will come to an end and
We have a new beginning
And a dream that people help each other when needed
I have a dream that there is no fear and no tears around
And I have a dream that people can say whatever
They want to and it comes out, always pleasant
Finally I have a dream that people share their
Feelings and money with each other.

**Nosheen Amin  (12)**
**Sowerby Bridge High School**


# A Dream I Could Grant!

*I have a dream!*
That I could move to Spain
Fly over on an aeroplane
Meet Spanish and English friends
But moving there, it all depends
My parents may not want to
They might have someone they want to cling on to
Every day after school
I'd jump in the pool!
Have a glass of water, or maybe some other refreshment
*I have a dream!*

**Olivia Stott  (12)**
**Sowerby Bridge High School**

# I Wish I Could Go On Holiday

I wish I could go on holiday for the first time
When I walk on the beach, I can feel the sand going through my toes
I can hear the children screaming with laughter as they break
                                    their sandcastles
I built a sandcastle and I had finished it and suddenly,
*Whoosh!* The waves wiped it out
I got some creamy ice cream and the taste was lovely
It was chocolate flavour and it was melting in my mouth
I could hear the seagulls chirping in the air as they flew
I ran into the water and I started splashing about
When suddenly a massive wave came and took me back to the sand
I was laughing.
*That was the best ride ever,* I said to myself.

**Tara Slater  (11)**
**Sowerby Bridge High School**


# The World Will Be Fine

I have a dream
That there are more houses and there is
Less money to buy
And that they are certain schools for different people
Who speak different languages

The world will be cool if it snowed for a
Week, month or even a year

Lessons will be fun if I could change the world
And I would make sure that there are no tests
The world will be fine if Christmas came more
Than once a year

I have a dream that we could go on computers
More in each lesson and have no homework
And me and my friends will stay friends forever.

*I have a dream.*

**Chloe Ross  (12)**
**Sowerby Bridge High School**

# I Wish About Heaven

I wish I was in Heaven
To see what it is like up there
The lovely angels singing
As I 'Rest In Peace'.

I wish the clouds were candyfloss
I'd eat them every day
Me too your bear-shaped candyfloss
Eaten every single day

To me the sky would be a swimming pool
I would swim in the sky
Every day
And have fun with my friends, even today

I would open the gates of Heaven
When my family and friends come by.

**Kerry Firth (12)**
**Sowerby Bridge High School**


# Chocolate

I wish the world was made of chocolate
I have a wish to eat my house. Oh, chocolate come
I have a wish to slurp on a chocolate bed
What is your dream?

Rich, smooth Galaxy melting on your tongue
Aero bubbles browsing in your mouth
What is your wish?

Dripping from every lamp post
You would see melting Mars Bars
You could eat anything you want
Even people or shops
What?

**Deanna Stephenson (12)**
**Sowerby Bridge High School**

# I Have A Dream

I have a dream
That people will live
Till they are hundreds of years old

People who are poor
Haven't got much food
Places like Africa
I dream of giving them so much more

People who haven't got money
May have to sleep in the street
To keep warm they may have to stamp their feet
Not much water when it is sunny

People who are poor
Haven't got much food
Places like Africa
I dream of giving them so much more

I have a dream of more water when the blazing sun
Is out which is as hot as a ball of fire
I have a dream of water which is as clear as crystal
Swishing and swaying from side to side

People who are poor
Haven't got much food
Places like Africa
I dream of giving them so much more.

**Sanober Mahmood  (12)**
**Sowerby Bridge High School**

# Just Think

What if
People stopped fighting
And started making peace?

What if
The world was a
World of happiness?

What if
There wasn't any
Violence or torture?

What if
Poverty didn't
Even exist?

What if
People stopped fussing
And just got on with
Their lives?

What if
Everybody could
Trust one another?

What if
People could turn
The other cheek
And start over?

Just think
What if all of this was true?
It helps to make a difference!

**Rebecca Waters (12)**
**West Leeds High School**

# Rosa Parks

Her heart was clean, full of rights
She never gave up, stayed brave and strong
Waved her speech across the world
Tried for 40 years, but never gave up

Always amiable and loving
Clean with the heart
Her hands were a weapon, always
There to help
Her brain was there always helping other people
Never doing something for herself

Stayed in jail, got arrested
But still worked hard
Got banned from buses
Still tried and tried, never gave up

Born in 1913
Died when she was 91
But sadly she is not with us right now
All her dreams came out to be true
Helped the blacks, gave them the freedom they
Actually needed
She had a clean heart and never had a misery

She always stayed intrepid and strong
Always fit and well
Some sorrowful news, she's not here today

She didn't stain their hearts
She didn't break their hearts.

**Natasha Naaz  (10)**
**Wycliffe CE Primary School**

# Mother Teresa

She created a world for the poor
Helpless and dying
She opened up her door
To the wounded and crying

Her body a reminder of an angel
The sky lit up with her face
As she walked the streets of Calcutta
In amazement and grace

She was sent down from the Heavens
Miraculous, wonderful, brave
Respected and a hero
To the people that she saved

Orphans did not exist
In the path that she walked
Babies were not abandoned
But loved and adored

We remember an astounding woman
Who is not with us today
She opened the eyes of Calcutta
And made a future for its days.

**Cristina Pacchiarini (11)**
**Wycliffe CE Primary School**